ACQUIRING CROSS-CULTURAL COMPETENCE

FOUR STAGES FOR STUDENTS OF FRENCH

ACQUIRING CROSS-CULTURAL COMPETENCE

FOUR STAGES FOR STUDENTS OF FRENCH

American Association of Teachers of French
National Commission on Cultural Competence

Howard L. Nostrand, Co-Chair
Allan W. Grundstrom, Co-Chair

Alan J. Singerman, Editor

National Textbook Company
a division of *NTC Publishing Group* • Lincolnwood, Illinois USA

© 1996 National Textbook Company, a division of NTC Publishing Group
4255 West Touhy Avenue, Lincolnwood (Chicago), Illinois 60646-1975 U.S.A.
All rights reserved.
No part of this book may be reproduced, stored in a retrieval system,
or transmitted in any form or by any means,
electronic, mechanical, photocopying, recording or otherwise,
without the prior permission of NTC Publishing Group.
Manufactured in the United States of America.

6 7 8 9 ML 0 9 8 7 6 5 4 3 2 1

COOPERATING ORGANIZATIONS

The following associations and agencies, engaged in developing standards to meet the national need for an effective cultural component, recommend that the definition of cultural competence as proposed in this report, as well as in parallel efforts, be considered in local planning. The cooperating organizations will continue to encourage attention to the cultural component by such means as announcing workshops and similar opportunities.

— The American Council on the Teaching of Foreign Languages.
  In reciprocal cooperation, ACTFL's National Standards in Foreign Language Education are applied here to French.
— The National Association of District Supervisors of Foreign Languages
— The American Association of Teachers of German
— The American Association of Teachers of Spanish and Portuguese
— The National French Contest of the American Association of Teachers of French
— The Language Acquisition Resource Center, San Diego State University
— The National Foreign Language Resource Center, University of Hawaii
— The Pacific Northwest Council on Foreign Languages
— The South Atlantic Modern Language Association
— The Southern Conference on Language Teaching
— The Southwest Conference on Language Teaching

CONTENTS

COOPERATING ORGANIZATIONS — v

INTRODUCTION:
TOWARD CONSENSUS ON A CORE OF CULTURAL COMPETENCE — 1
(Howard Nostrand)

ACKNOWLEDGMENTS — 7

CULTURAL COMPETENCE CHART — 8

PART I.
UNDERSTANDING CULTURE — 9
    A. Empathy Toward Other Cultures *(Claire Kramsch, Pauline Nelson)* — 11
    B. Ability to Observe and Analyze a Culture
       (Alain Ranwez, Ann Williams-Gascon) — 14

PART II.
KNOWLEDGE OF FRENCH-SPEAKING SOCIETIES — 17
    A. France *(Marie-Christine Koop, Tom Carr)* — 19
    ▓ An Inventory of the French Value System
       (Howard Nostrand, Claudette Imberton-Hunt) — 26
    B. French-Speaking North America *(Paul Barrette)* — 32
    C. French-Speaking Sub-Saharan Africa *(Charles Hancock, Lauren Yoder)* — 38
    D. The French-Speaking Caribbean *(Charles Hancock, Lauren Yoder)* — 46
    E. French-Speaking North Africa *(Jawed Zouari)* — 50

PART III.
GRADES 9 THROUGH 12 *(Ali Moeller, Renée White)* — 57

PART IV.
KINDERGARTEN THROUGH EIGHTH GRADE *(Katherine Kurk)* — 65

PART V.
TESTING CULTURAL COMPETENCE *(Walter Bartz, Rosalie Vermette)* — 75

APPENDIX I
To Find Time For Both Language and Culture *(Howard Nostrand)* — 85

APPENDIX II
Toward A Deeper Understanding of the French Value System
(Howard Nostrand) — 89

BIBLIOGRAPHIES *(Louise Damen)*	**97**
A. Communication in Cultural Context	97
B. Skills of Observation and Analysis	98
C. Empathy Toward Other Cultures	100
D. French-Speaking Areas: General	101
E. 1. France: General	103
2. The French Value System	107
3. France and Europe	108
F. French-Speaking North America	109
G. French-Speaking Sub-Saharan Africa and the Caribbean	114
H. French-Speaking North Africa	116
I. English-Speaking United States	117
J. Foreign Languages and Intercultural Education	119
K. Integrating Language and Culture	121
L. Adaptation to Grades K–8 and 9–12	123
M. Testing and Evaluation	128

INTRODUCTION

TOWARD CONSENSUS ON A CORE OF CULTURAL COMPETENCE

—Howard L. Nostrand, with grateful acknowledgment to our many contributing colleagues

This introduction owes its existence to the language teachers and administrators whose critiques from diverse theoretical and practical perspectives have shaped the successive drafts of this book. Other thoughtful colleagues will have the same concerns as they: Why a structured cultural component? And why consensus on a concerted effort? The following introductory remarks are an attempt to answer those questions.

The Present Need: National and Individual

The rising importance of cross-cultural communication and understanding in the modern world has generated a new need, and language teachers have shown their ability to respond to it, not only by aiming at communicative competence but by reversing their attitude toward "the culture." A half-century ago, the predominant reaction of teachers in a regional or national meeting was one of anger: "Do you want me to be an anthropologist, too? I have enough to do!" World War II had just begun to show that communicative competence has a cultural component: the anthropologist Henry Lee Smith, working with the Army Specialized Training Program, found that the ASTP had produced trainees so proficient in Spanish, yet so unprepared for the culture, that their hosts thought they were being deliberately insulted!

A decade ago, when language and culture came to be widely reognized as inseparable, the dominant reaction changed to "Yes, I bring in the culture"; but that has usually meant incidental fragments. Students have grown interested in the culture for a variety of reasons, some because trade-related jobs pay better, some because of experience with cultural conflict between generations. Interest in the culture has become an important incentive for studying literature. Clearly, the time has come to integrate language and culture into an effective communicative competence.

Today the American public, the business community, and the political leadership of left and right agree that "competitiveness" abroad is urgent; they also agree that ethnic and ideological conflicts at home weaken democracy. Ethnic conflict affects economic productivity as employers recruit workers from a culturally diverse labor pool, and management contends with distrust between ethnic groups. The need today is not only for persons who can communicate and negotiate across cultural barriers, but for citizens in all walks of life who can play constructive roles in managing cultural divisiveness. This divisiveness is clearly a problem for education, and American education at present is not successful in coping with it. The urgency of the need is evident. The problem is to find forces to meet it.

An Appropriate Role for a Second Language and Culture

This discipline has a unique potential for strengthening this weak area of education. Its uniqueness is that it alone brings into mutual reinforcement three basic elements of education and applies them to cross-cultural understanding.

The first element is *cognitive:* in this field, the knowledge of how a culture makes sense only in its own terms. Translation, on the contrary, distorts and transforms an intended meaning as it converts to the terms of a different culture. The second element is *affective:* in this case, the experience of sensing how values, customs, and human relations are felt when they are perceived through a different grid of meanings. The third element is *behavioral:* here, the experience of making one's own the intonations, body language and social proprieties which at first one tends to caricature. For example, the superficial reaction "They are always shaking hands!" yields to an understanding of how the French individualize interpersonal relations. It is by making one's own what was "other," that one can extend one's capacity for understanding beyond the wall of ethnocentrism. Understanding, after all, has been well defined as "knowledge deepened by experience." This is why the mutual reinforcement is so important.

Given the need to strengthen intercultural education, the unique potential of this discipline should certainly be made as effective as possible. Our effectiveness will be subjected to "accountability" when the "Goals 2000" program begins the nation-wide testing in a foreign language at grades 4, 8, and 12 among the other "basic subjects" of the curriculum. If a narrowly conceived language proficiency alone were offered as the justification for the inclusion of this field, the support of the public, business, and government would remain as lukewarm as it has been.

A meaningful grasp of a language and its culture requires a long learning process, efficient sequencing, and consequently, a concerted effort of teachers and curriculum builders from the elementary grades through college. Research beginning with John B. Carroll in the 1960s (see Bibliography L) confirms the advantage of an early beginning. An effective sequence has the further advantage of motivating students to continue their French, by offering them a coherent succession of challenges in place of what they too often find: a ladder with missing rungs or a treadmill. But this further benefit, also, depends on a working consensus among the teachers and supporting educators, as students move from grade to grade, and as so many of them move from town to town.

Consensus on a Feasible Objective: A Common Core at Four Sucessive Levels

Consensus is needed on a minimal core which *must* leave time for individual interests. These are essential for the first two of the ten devices that may make room for both language and culture, discussed in Appendix I. The Commission was relieved to discover that consensus is necessary only on *defining* the core competence, not on *designing* its pedagogical applications: there, the strength of the profession lies in its diversity. Indeed, the same is true of the language. And consensus here is not the usual problem of reconciling conflicting self-interests, but simply one of effectively serving a shared interest: namely, to meet a recognized need and thereby win respect for this discipline. All language teachers certainly want to develop the abilities and understanding most likely to prove of lasting value to their students.

What is needed, then, is not a prescription of what to teach, but an organizer, a check list of suggestive "indicators" defining the tasks the learner should become capable of performing. This requires defining successive stages, for a feasible objective must be articulated into segments in order to avoid overwhelming the learner, and also to permit building upon a well-laid basis. The American Council on the Teaching of Foreign Languages (ACTFL) has already developed just such a check list for language competence: the *Proficiency Guidelines*. The present volume proposes to define the cultural tasks which complete the ability to communicate effectively.

ACTFL uses the term "Levels" of language proficiency. The term "Stages" is proposed for the cultural component, so as to avoid suggesting a closer correlation than is possible. But the successive sets of linguistic and cultural tasks are related closely enough so that the teaching can be integrated and the two components can reinforce each other. ACTFL subdivides the first segments from "Low" to "High." The cultural stages simply indicate the competence to be attained by the end of the segment.

Stage 1, "Elementary," defines the cultural tasks related to the Novice level. It emphasizes observation and imitation, with some progress toward the development of basic practical intercultural skills in the target culture.

Stage 2, "Basic intercultural skills" (cf. the Intermediate level) defines the skills and supporting knowledge necessary to meet one's basic needs in the foreign society, together with a rudimentary understanding of its most prominent cultural phenomena.

Stage 3, "Social competence" (cf. the Advanced level) assumes the ability to function appropriately in a wide variety of social situations and a more thorough knowledge and understanding of cultural phenomena.

Stage 4, "Socioprofessional capability" (cf. the Superior level) denotes both in-depth cultural knowledge and the skills, understanding, and sensitivity adequate for full socioprofessional responsibility (an attainment which lies beyond the usual undergraduate program).

Future research into the functional needs for each set of tasks may shift some of the proposed indicators from one Stage to another, but meanwhile, collective experience permits far more than snap judgments.

The Commission recommends that Stage 1 be the principal focus in K–8. Students in accelerated FLES* curricula, such as partial or total immersion programs, can advance well into Stage 2. For students who begin the study of French in high school, Stage 1 is considered the normal level of achievement for grades 9–10, and Stage 2 for grades 11 and 12. High school students in accelerated French programs, like Advanced Placement or the International Baccalaureat, can begin some of the tasks of Stage 3, and college students who study for a year or more in a French-speaking country may master parts of Stage 4. Separate chapters in this book provide for adapting the indicators of cultural competence to both K–8 and grades 9–12. At the least, all French students should complete Stage 2 in college. Stage 3 should be the norm for those majoring in French and for the beginning teacher, Stage 4 for the master teacher and national certification.

The Basis for a Broadening Consensus

The characteristic Western method of solving a complex problem is to advance by successive approximations, often an exciting adventure and indeed so in this case. The goal is to define a common core which can satisfy the language-teaching profession and its supporting educators, and can meet the more demanding challenge of the need. The framework presented in this volume is far from the first approximation and doubtless far from the last.

The background of the present result is useful for building upon it. The most instructive part begins in 1982, with the sections on culture in the ACTFL *Provisional Guidelines,* an adaptation of the standards which had been developed, notably, by the U.S. Government's Interagency Language Roundtable (ILR), as qualifications for foreign assignments. The adaptation to school use required a less specialized competence and thus the insertion of a "Novice" Level, since the "survival" level of the foreign operative was too much for a beginner. The 1982 draft proved impractical, especially for testing such as is done in the ACTFL Oral Proficiency Interview. During the 1980s several published and unpublished revisions were circulated for criticism, resulting in a much improved draft which identified the ten issues to be addressed by this Commission.

In 1992, the first sixty teachers and administrators from schools and colleges who agreed to take part in the Commission's work were divided into ten groups. Two groups dealt with the affective capacity for empathy and the question of what one needs to know in order to observe and analyze a culture effectively, now the sections of Part I. Five other groups undertook to develop reasonable goals regarding knowledge of the main French-speaking areas, including behavioral sociolinguistic ability—the present Part II of this work. Two additional groups adapted the description of the college/adult competence to lower age levels, grades K–8 and 9–12, and the last one addressed the problem of testing. During the subsequent three years, the findings of the work groups led to significant changes in the evolving framework for cultural competence, as described below.

The seven categories of knowledge found necessary for understanding a culture area made it evident that all of French-speaking Europe was too big an area for the core competence. The proposed solution limits the European core to France, while new groups of Belgian and Swiss specialists develop supplemental units to encourage interested learners. This volume also presents sets of indicators of cultural competence for French-speaking North America (Quebec especially), Sub-Saharan Africa, the Caribbean, and North Africa. Another new group is developing indicators for French-speaking societies of Southeast Asia and the Pacific as an additional option, but the present study does not attempt to be all-inclusive in this first concerted effort to establish a model for measuring cultural competence.

In one of the meetings of Commission members held at national conventions, the group coordinators for the culture areas concluded that the heterogeneous surface manifestations they were encountering required some organizing structure to make the materials manageable. This led to agreement that the most important common values should be one of the seven categories of cultural knowledge. An inventory of the French value system, whose essential background is examined in Appendix II, was therefore added to the section on France (Part II.A).

The adaptation of the college/adult objectives to childhood and adolescence proved to require quite different sets of learner tasks, based on those stages of human development and on coordination with the concomitant school subjects.

Lastly, the sharpened differentiation between *defining* the core competence and *designing* strategies resulted in a Canadian–U.S. Committee charged with compiling a Repertory of

Pedagogical Applications—a resource needed by teachers in both countries, which may be housed eventually in one of the Canadian databases on Francophone cultures.

The Substance of a Core Competence

The core consists of behavioral skills, cognitive abilities, and the affective capacity for dealing with intercultural differences in a constructive spirit. As a teacher plans a unit of instruction it is useful to consider separately its behavioral, cognitive and affective possibilities; but the separation disappears in the composite learning experience that results.

The skills are determined by the behavior acceptable from a foreigner—indeed, better than "acceptable," behavior that elicits good will. Laurence Wylie has defined the non-verbal part of congenial interaction (see Bibliography A). "Skill" must be broadly conceived as an ability supported by knowledge of why some behavior patterns meet with a positive response and others are detrimental. For example, the slang that students are so eager to practice may be perceived as aggressive coming from an outsider to a group which has not invited such familiarity.

The requisite knowledge includes an understanding of the culture patterns one is likely to encounter, and the ability to observe and analyze these patterns for oneself. There are more than 40 French-speaking areas, but it is proposed that a sufficient core may be limited to a knowledge of one main area, guided by the descriptors in Part II, plus an informed interest in one other and an awareness of the rest of the main areas. Modest knowledge of any one non-European area can overcome the narrowness of Eurocentrism, and just an awareness of the rest is enough to enrich the learner's subsequent experience of world events. Attention to the impact of French culture on the former colonies and protectorates can make this widely useful Western language a window on the Third World and a source of motivation for African-American, Asian, and other students not spontaneously interested in Europe.

As students move from school to school they will find that different culture areas have been selected. But these areas have enough underlying similarities so that what each newcomer brings to the class can broaden the understanding of all. The descriptions of the areas facilitate comparison by focussing on how each area differs from France.

The knowledge of how to observe and analyze a culture, and the capacity for empathy, are of course the same for all culture areas. Ways of observing and analyzing for oneself can be taught, and can make the learner's experience much more rewarding than unassisted trial and error. Observation and analysis are both made more productive by the fascinating conceptual tools proposed in the works by Edward T. Hall (see Bibliography B). One way to focus observation is to examine the misunderstandings that arise at the points of contact between two cultures, an approach which is illustrated in Raymonde Carroll's *Evidences invisibles,* published in both French and English (see Bibliography A).

Analysis differs from observation. Surface manifestations can be described with relative certainty, while explanations must remain open-ended because we may have overlooked some causal factor. But observing and analyzing both inevitably involve generalizing as we strive to make sense of raw experience, and as we observe, we should recognize when we are generalizing. Examples and anecdotes fascinate precisely because they seem to be typical of something, yet they lead to unwarranted stereotypes unless they exemplify a statistically valid generalization. "Authentic examples" do not protect one against inauthentic generalizing.

Analysis involves the ability not only to recognize but to criticize generalizations. Textbooks should be expected to tell at least the date of an opinion poll and the population surveyed. When subgroups are compared, moreover, the expert critic wants to know whether the sample was adequate. In our culture, comfortable with concrete things but not with abstractions, learning to criticize generalizations has to overcome a tendency to regard them as concrete products. The *process* of generalizing needs to be taught, and here the study of a culture gives ideal practice in critical thinking.

Confusion results from the failure to realize that there are three very different levels of useful generalization: about the needs and aspirations common to all humanity, about cultures, and about individuals. Focussing exclusively on the mid-level has led to an obsessive overemphasis on intercultural differences. Attention to the universals is a main resource for the essential intercultural skill of finding common ground and appealing to shared interests, aspirations and concerns. Attention to the bottom level, individual differences, avoids putting too much trust in the predictive power of generalizations about a culture.

The third part of cultural competence, after the skills and knowledge, is the affective capacity for empathy, first of all toward the target culture, and a resulting insight into one's own culture. The fostering of empathy involves the problem of eliciting attitudes without imposing them. Indoctrination can, and must, be avoided at all age levels. In childhood education, the teacher need only set the example of intellectual curiosity and the resolve to understand what is "other." In later years, thoughtful discussion encourages empathetic attitudes by exposing and discrediting stereotypes. The values for which students want to be known prove to favor the attitudes which elicit good will and are conducive to a positive cross-cultural experience.

Unlike other aspects of cultural competence, the outcome of empathy cannot be broken down into a sequence of successive objectives. Its dominant affective element has no simple form that can be taught first as Stage 1. It is a feeling inherently complex. Moreover, the fragile ability to accept what is "other" conflicts from the start with the ethnocentrism on which our feeling of security depends—until we learn otherwise. And we cannot postpone the most difficult, complex occasions for empathy that arise in real life: racial antagonism, irritating social customs, contradictory beliefs. The solution lies in the clear distinction between the affective element which is dominant in empathy, and the cognitive and behavioral elements which support it. These latter kinds of learning, as Part I of this book will show, can be sequenced, and they can be tested as well.

It is important to realize, finally, that the study of a foreign culture can result in insight into one's own culture. This is well illustrated by the effect of discovering the diverse perspectives inherent in a culture with a colonial past. "La Francophonie," for example, means for France the possibility of remaining more than a local European power. For the Afro-French identity it means memories of colonialism. For Quebec, on the contrary, it is the safeguard of ethnic identity. One is led to inquire how one's own attitudes have been shaped by history.

In sum, it is possible to learn an art of living amidst a plurality of cultures, analyzing differences in a dispassionate spirit of intellectual curiosity, discovering common ground and appealing to shared purposes, and conforming abroad to the customs of a foreign society while remaining culturally one's own person.

ACKNOWLEDGMENTS

In addition to the coordinators of each section of this book—the prime movers in each area—dozens of colleagues across the country have contributed invaluable expertise to the development of this framework for cultural competence. While it is impossible to recognize everyone who made comments or suggestions, the Co-Chairs and Editor would like to express their most heartfelt thanks to those colleagues who helped shape the debate and/or lent particularly significant support to the work of this Commission in accomplishing its goals. Jayne Abrate *(Univ. of Missouri-Rolla)*, Wendy Allen *(Saint Olaf College, MN)*, Evelyne Armstrong *(Charles Wright Academy, WA)*, Denise Asfar *(Educational Testing Service, Princeton, NJ)*, Claudine Bénétreau *(Collège "Les Bouvets", Puteaux, France)*, Marc Boucher *(Director, Bureau du Québec, Atlanta)*, Eloise Brière *(SUNY-Albany)*, Paul Bowles *(Tangier, Morocco)*, Raymonde Carroll *(Oberlin College)*, Christie Cibulsky *(Newton-Conover City Schools, NC)*, Helen Cummings *(Boston Public Schools)*, Louise Damen *(Univ. of So. Florida, retired)*, Mary De Lopez *(Univ. of Texas)*, Martha Dobson *(Iredell-Statesville Schools, NC)*, Charles Dockery *(Davidson College)*, Phyllis Dragonas *(Melrose Public Schools, MA)*, Patrica Duggar *(Paul Breaux Middle School, LA)*, Virginia Gramer *(Monroe School, IL)*, Hector Hammerly *(Simon Fraser Univ., British Columbia)*, Mary Kimball *(Pacific University)*, Edward Knox *(Middlebury College)*, Marie-Pierre Koban *(Lakeside School, WA)*, Robert Lafayette *(Louisiana State Univ.)*, Anna Lambros *(Georgia State Univ.)*, Rolande Leguillon *(Univ. of St. Thomas, TX)*, David Long *(Memorial H.S., TX)*, Eileen Lorenz *(Montgomery County Public Schools, MD)*, Pardee Lowe, Jr. *(Interagency Language Roundtable)*, Julie Maddox *(Latonia Elementary School, KY)*, Myriam Met *(Montgomery County Public Schools, MD)*, Anne Nietert *(Newton-Conover City Schools, NC)*, Gladys Lipton *(Univ. of Maryland, Baltimore County)*, Constantina Mitchell *(Gallaudet Univ., Wash. D.C.)*, Chris Pinet *(Montana State Univ.)*, Claire Quintal *(Assumption College, MA)*, Sharon Rapp *(Conway H.S., AR)*, June Philipps *(Weber State Univ.)*, Susan Redd *(Mount Vernon H.S., WA)*, Gail Robinson *(San Diego State Univ.)*, Michèle Shockey *(Gunn H.S., CA)*, Roland Simon *(Univ. of Virginia)*, Ross Steele *(Univ. of Sydney, New South Wales, Australia)*, Andrew Suozzo *(DePaul Univ.)*, Jerry Toussaint *(Dept. of Public Instruction, NC)*, Rebecca Valette *(Boston College)*, Jacqueline Viswanathan *(Simon Fraser Univ., British Columbia)*, and Dale Wallace *(Newton-Conover City Schools, NC)*.

CULTURAL COMPETENCE CHART

UNDERSTANDING CULTURE
Empathy Toward Other Cultures

Ability to Observe and Analyze a Culture

KNOWLEDGE OF FRENCH-SPEAKING SOCIETIES

Focus on 5 areas
- France
- North America
- Sub-Saharan Africa
- The Caribbean
- North Africa

7 Categories of Cultural Knowledge
- Communication in Cultural Context
- The Value System
- Social Patterns and Conventions
- Social Institutions
- Geography and the Environment
- History
- Literature and the Arts

LEVELS OF COMPETENCE
Stage 1: Elementary

Stage 2: Basic Intercultural Skills

Stage 3: Social Competence

Stage 4: Socioprofessional Capability

PART I

UNDERSTANDING CULTURE

This section includes a) Empathy Toward Other Cultures and b) the Ability to Observe and Analyze a Culture. These two areas of competency have in common their general nature (i.e. their relevance to all target cultures), as opposed to the culture-specific character of Part III dealing with knowledge about French-speaking societies.

 EMPATHY TOWARD OTHER CULTURES

Coordinators: Claire Kramsch, University of California, Berkeley
Pauline Nelson, Bethany College, West Virginia

Empathy, an informed openness toward other cultures, is an essential element of cultural competence, promoting both fruitful intercultural relations and the development of an insightful and objective perspective on one's own culture. It underlies the acquisition of cultural competence from beginning to end, for students must first be open to other cultures before they can assimilate and use cultural knowledge, while the development of cultural competence itself leads to greater empathy toward the target culture.

Like all learning that involves attitudes, empathy has three elements: affective, cognitive, and behavioral. But empathy differs from other components of cultural competence in that here the affective element is dominant; empathy is above all an attitude. This peculiarity of empathy makes a difference in the way it has to be learned and taught: the development of affective qualities cannot be correlated with the progressive acquisition of either linguistic skills or cultural knowledge. The development of open and accepting attitudes toward people who are different may precede the acquisition of simple linguistic skills and cultural knowledge, whereas superior linguistic ability and cultural knowledge may not be accompanied by a very great empathy.

We present below, in a progressive sequence, the cognitive and behavioral components which support and promote the dominant affective element of empathy.

INDICATORS OF COMPETENCE

Upon completing STAGE 1, the learner:
- is curious about similarities and differences between the home and the target culture.
- shows willingness to understand the differences encountered.

Upon completing STAGE 2, the learner:
- is tolerant of differences between the home and target culture.
- is open and accepting of different peoples.
- recognizes the depth and complexity of cultural differences.
- shows an active interest in the search for understanding of the target culture.

Upon completing STAGE 3, the learner:

- is aware of the problem of accepting the norms of another culture while maintaining one's own values and identity.
- shows fair-mindedness and tolerance in trying to solve an embarrassing situation or a cross-cultural conflict.
- can adjust behavior and conversation according to the situational context and to the expectations of participants.

Upon completing STAGE 4, the learner:

- recognizes the importance of understanding manifestations of the target culture in terms of its own context.
- is aware of his/her own cultural perspective and of how this perspective influences one's perception of phenomena.
- can act and react in a culturally appropriate way while being aware of his/her "otherness".

An Example of Stages of Empathy Based on the French Admiration of Logic and their Penchant for Reasoned Discussion and Debate

Joe Johnson, an American visiting France, is confronted in social situations with much more verbal disagreement and argumentation than is customary back home. He would be expected to exhibit, more or less, the following reactions according to his level of empathy:

Stage 1: Unaccustomed to aggressive disagreement in social conversation, Joe finds the French argumentative and perhaps hostile or anti-American. He overcomes an initial negative reaction and tries to understand an apparent cultural difference.

Stage 2: Joe has listened to discussions among the French and has come to understand the importance and frequency of lively intellectual discussion and debate. He recognizes his own discomfort in the face of disagreement, and his lack of experience with this kind of conversation, to be cultural phenomena.

Stage 3: Joe has adopted the distinction made in French culture between the opposition of ideas and the opposition of people. He makes an effort to become better informed on topics likely to be discussed in the French environment and seeks to participate in discussions appropriately. Recognizing the differences in American and French conversation styles, he accepts that his own behavior may have to be different in each culture and explores how far he is willing to go to conform.

Stage 4: Joe is willing to adjust behavior in order to be an active, respected, and comfortable participant in discussions in both cultures. He accepts the differences in approach to conversation and debate, without judging them as either right or wrong.

Pedagogical Tasks

Pedagogical tasks designed to nurture and reinforce empathy can likewise be arranged in a sequence from lesser to greater complexity. Such tasks, which can both promote empathy and provide a basis for evaluation, can be conceived in such a manner as to facilitate the learner's development toward greater cultural sophistication in each area, as is suggested in the following grid:

1. *Cognitive tasks:* **The learner progresses**
   — from situation-specific knowledge to relational thinking.
   — from factual knowledge to conceptualization.
   — from fixed rules of use to variable rules of use.
   — from equating of native and target culture concepts to dissociation of same.

2. *Affective tasks:* **The learner progresses**
   — from exclusively native culture-centered perspective to target culture-centered.
   — from true/false concepts to awareness of multiple truths.
   — from tolerance of difference to relativizing self and other.

3. *Behavioral tasks:* **The learner progresses**
   — from reproduction of specific situations to the quest for comparable ones.
   — from obligatory contexts of use to variable contexts of use.
   — from ability to function in provided contexts to the ability to create contexts.
   — from little or no interaction to high degree of interaction.

It should be noted, finally, that the evidences of empathy are part of a psychological ensemble, or *Gestalt,* which must be developed and tested as a whole as much as possible. The manifestations of empathy which cannot be tested in a written test or an oral proficiency interview can be evaluated by other means, such as role-playing or a portfolio.

 # ABILITY TO OBSERVE AND ANALYZE A CULTURE

Coordinators: Alain Ranwez and Ann Williams-Gascon
Metropolitan State College of Denver

As we strive to learn and to teach about cultures, we are faced with a seemingly endless stream of information. This "cultural overload" can lead to stereotyping and overgeneralizing as we attempt to grasp and to explain a target culture and the difference between that culture and our own. Generalizations about other cultures seem inevitable and can be useful, of course, if they are seen as hypotheses to be confirmed rather than instant truths. A valid interpretation of cultural phenomena normally involves, at the very least, a two-step process: first observation, then analysis. One of the most important skills that we can cultivate in ourselves and in our students is thus the ability both to observe the target culture in an informed manner and to analyze judiciously the results of that observation.

INDICATORS OF COMPETENCE

Upon completing STAGE 1, the learner:

— can give examples of the relationship between language and culture (e.g., different forms of oral address, depending on social relations and situation).

— can identify a few characteristics of the target culture as cultural patterns (e.g., businesses and government offices in France may close for as long as two hours at lunch time).

— can identify a few common cultural differences between home and target cultures (e.g., the presentation of American and French meals).

— can identify some commonly-held images of the target culture as stereotypes (e.g., "the French drink wine with their meals").

Upon completing STAGE 2, the learner:

— can demonstrate understanding that cultural values, patterns, and institutions cannot be used to predict the behavior of all individuals (e.g., not all French people avoid creating relations with their neighbors to preserve their privacy).

— can give examples of an observer's own cultural biases interfering with understanding of the target culture (e.g., being embarrassed by kissing on the cheek between female friends in France).
— can give an example of how cultures change over time (e.g., in some workplaces in France the noon meal time has been shortened considerably).
— can discuss ways in which cultural norms and values are transmitted (e.g., the role of parents as models and teachers of values).
— can give examples of one culture influencing another (e.g., the popularity of American-style fast-food restaurants in France).

Upon completing STAGE 3, the learner:

— can give examples of social behaviors that express the target culture's underlying value system (e.g., the reluctance of French people to invite casual acquaintances into their homes is an expression of their concept of friendship, their value of privacy, and their general distrust of outsiders).
— can describe and explain important elements of major institutions in the target culture (e.g., can describe the baccalaureat exam and its importance in the French educational system).
— can interpret social phenomena within the context of the target culture (e.g., understands how the frequent recourse to public demonstrations in France is related to administrative centralization).
— can describe several instances of major change within the target culture (e.g., fewer and fewer French people attend religious services regularly).
— can describe some major forces that influence culture and cultural change (e.g., the role of technology: the Minitel, television, etc.).
— recognizes that a culture is not uniform and can identify the principal subcultures of the target culture (e.g., the increasing importance of Moslem culture in France).

Upon completing STAGE 4, the learner:

— can critique phenomena of the target culture with a minimum of bias (e.g., can discuss the various political parties in France objectively, whether on the "left" or on the "right").
— can interpret social phenomena at several levels of generalization (e.g., can discuss the development of the role of women in the world, in France in general, and in a given French social class).
— can decribe the multifaceted character of sociocultural phenomena (e.g., the historical, social, religious, economic, and political dimensions of the growing North African population in France).

PART II

KNOWLEDGE OF FRENCH-SPEAKING SOCIETIES

Cultural competence necessarily includes specific knowledge of the target culture. The framework proposed in this report includes knowledge not only of France but also, in order to transcend the traditional Eurocentric cultural perspective, of four other major French-speaking areas or communities: **North America** (with an emphasis on Quebec), **Sub-Saharan Africa, the Caribbean, and North Africa** (the Maghreb). Teachers and students are not expected to be knowledgeable in all of these cultures. In addition to the study of France, however, teachers are encouraged to begin challenging students as early as possible with some Stage 1 tasks in the knowledge of at least one other French-speaking area. The Commission recognizes that there are other important Francophone societies than those represented here, in Europe as well as in Southeast Asia and the Pacific, but does not attempt to be all-inclusive in this first effort to establish a comprehensive model for measuring cultural competence. Working groups are being established, however, to provide similar sets of knowledge indicators for French-speaking Switzerland and Belgium, as well as other Francophone cultures around the globe.

Indicators of knowledge of each of the five areas represented are grouped under **seven cultural categories**: "Communication in Cultural Context," "The Value System," "Social Patterns and Conventions," "Social Institutions," "Geography and the Environment," "History," and "Literature and the Arts". This organization is intended both to lend insight into the major aspects of cultural knowledge and to provide a coherent and systematic framework for the sequencing of goals through the four stages. While some of the above categories are self-evident, others deserve a word of explanation.

The first of the categories, **"Communication in Cultural Context,"** refers to the importance of knowing what to say and how to say it appropriately in various social situations. Since familiarity with the styles, variations, and codes of a culture is fundamental to effective communication, this category groups together indicators of sociolinguistic abilities which address this area of competence. In addition to variations in verbal language according to specific cultural contexts, this area encompasses non-verbal elements of communication. These include conversational distances between speakers ("proxemics"), as well as gestures, facial expressions, and body movement ("kinesics"), and some meaningful sounds which are not themselves words ("paralanguage").

The "**Value System**," inventoried at the end of the section on France, refers to the set of slowly evolving **highest common values** (i.e., values which are not subordinated to other values)—colored by a context of **characteristic thought patterns** and **prevalent assumptions about human nature and society**—whose knowledge facilitates the understanding of the surface manifestations of that system encountered in French social patterns, institutions, and forms of artistic expression.

The categories of **"Social Patterns and Conventions"** and **"Social Institutions"** both deal with the organized relations of people in society, although in different ways. Social patterns and conventions are unofficial patterns of collective behavior, including such phenomena as social hierarchy and mobility, sex roles, age-group and ethnic relations, the counterculture, etiquette, letter-writing formalities, traditional dishes and menus, and common public signs. Social institutions are more official structures, often codified in law, including civil status, religion, education, political processes, government, economic structures, labor and professional unions, currency, health care, and artistic and scientific organizations.

The indicators of competence for the non-European French-speaking communities focus on those cultural features which are different from those in France. It is understood, however, that each of these communities share certain sociocultural features (e.g., the educational system) with continental France.

FRANCE

*Coordinators: Marie-Christine Koop, University of North Texas
Tom Carr, University of Nebraska-Lincoln*

INDICATORS OF COMPETENCE

Upon completing STAGE 1, the learner:

Communication in Cultural Context
— knows what verbal behavior is appropriate in different greeting and leave-taking routines (e.g., "Bonjour, Madame" vs. "Salut, Jean").
— knows that there are familiar and polite forms of address ("tu" vs. "vous").
— recognizes some easily interpreted gestures (e.g., hand-waving in greetings or leave-taking, crossing of the arms, cupping the ear).
— is aware of differences in demeanor in formal and informal social settings (e.g., having a drink in a café among friends vs. dining with a French friend's family).

The Value System
Competence in this category begins at Stage 2.

Social Patterns and Conventions
— can describe the basic conventions governing greeting and leave-taking as regards the age and sex of those being greeted and social relationships (e.g., a handshake vs. kissing on the cheek).
— can identify some common foods (e.g., the baguette, crêpes, cheeses, wines, crème caramel).
— can say which kinds of specialized stores sell what kinds of merchandise (e.g., bread is bought in a "boulangerie," stamps at the post office or in a "bureau de tabac").
— can describe daily meal patterns (scheduling of lunch and dinner).
— can describe the order of dishes served in a traditional meal.
— can describe the functions of the different rooms in a typical dwelling (e.g., "les WC" as opposed to "la salle de bains").

Social Institutions
— is familiar with basic measurements used in France (e.g., metric system, French currency, 24-hour clock, Celsius thermometer).

— can name major modes of public transportation (e.g., "métro," taxi, bus, train and "TGV").
— can name the major school levels from the "maternelle" to the "lycée" and knows the corresponding ages of the students.
— recognizes the French national anthem and knows it is called "La Marseillaise."
— can identify the French flag.

Geography and the Environment
— can find France on a map of Europe.
— can place on an outline map of France the principal mountain ranges, rivers, and surrounding bodies of water.
— can state the relative size of France (e.g., roughly as large as Texas).
— can state the approximate population of France as compared to the U.S.
— can locate on an outline map some of the other countries where French is spoken in Europe.

History
— can name and identify from their pictures five major historical landmarks and monuments of Paris (e.g., Notre-Dame de Paris, Sainte Chapelle, Madeleine, Palais du Luxembourg, Palais du Louvre, Invalides, Panthéon, Arc de Triomphe, Obélisque, Sacré-Coeur, Tour Eiffel, Centre Pompidou).
— can name and identify from their pictures five major historical landmarks and monuments of France outside of Paris (e.g., Versailles, Pont du Gard, Mont-Saint-Michel, une cathédrale gothique, un grand château de la Loire, la Place Stanislas de Nancy, Lourdes).

Literature and the Arts
— can identify several important French authors, artists, and/or composers (e.g., Racine, Mme de Lafayette, Voltaire, Balzac, Hugo, Sartre, Ravel, Manet, Rodin, Morisot, Camille Claudel, le douanier Rousseau).
— can recognize some popular folk songs (e.g., "Chevaliers de la Table Ronde," "Auprès de ma blonde").

Upon completing STAGE 2, the learner:

Communication in Cultural Context
— uses appropriate titles of address and formulas in survival-level situations (e.g., "S'il vous plaît" to call a waiter).
— can use familiar and polite forms of address ("tu" vs. "vous") appropriately.
— demonstrates knowledge of some common formulas used in communications (e.g., beginning and ending letters, answering the telephone).
— is aware of the difference in conversational distance in the U.S.A. and in France (i.e., that the French feel comfortable at a closer distance than is customary for Americans).

The Value System
— can identify at least three of the highest common values and two mental habits in the value context. (See Inventory at the end of this section.)

— can recognize some manifestations of the above.
— is able to give at least one example of the difference between French and American values (e.g., the concepts of friendship or patriotism).

Social Patterns and Conventions
— can describe principal differences in table manners in France and in the U.S.
— knows the importance of the handshake in greeting and leave-taking.
— can describe several social conventions of the youth culture (e.g., going out with a group of friends rather than "dating," meeting at cafés and "crêperies," going to "boums" or "soirées").
— knows the importance of the evening meal as a family tradition.
— can identify the chief regional subcultures in France (e.g., Alsatian, Basque, Breton, etc.).
— can identify the ethnic origins of the most prominent groups of recent immigrants (e.g., North African, Portuguese, etc.).

Social Institutions
— knows the basics of travel in France (e.g., using public transportation and communications, changing currencies, securing lodgings, ordering a meal from a restaurant menu).
— can name the major religious and civil holidays and explain how they are celebrated (e.g., Labor Day, July 14, All Saints Day, Armistice Day, Christmas).
— can describe several kinds of family structures common in France (e.g., "cellulaire, étendue, monoparentale").
— can describe elements of student life at primary and secondary levels of education (e.g., elitism, teachers as authority figures, discipline).
— can name the current president and prime minister of France.
— can name at least half of the countries in the European Union.

Geography and the Environment
— can place the main cities of France on an outline map.
— can place the principal geographical regions of France on an outline map (e.g., "Bassin parisien, Massif Central, Loire Valley," etc.).
— can place the French-speaking areas of Belgium and Switzerland (Wallonie, Suisse romande) on an outline map.

History
— can identify an important event in each of the major periods (Middle Ages, 16th cen., 17th cen., etc.) of the history of France (e.g., "Guerre de Cent Ans, Edit de Nantes, Révolution, Occupation, Mai '68").
— can identify at least one prominent historical personality linked to each of the above events (e.g., respectively, Jeanne d'Arc, Henri IV, Louis XVI, Pétain, De Gaulle).

Literature and the Arts
— can identify at least three major authors, each from a different historical period, and at least one work by each (e.g., Chrétien de Troyes, *Lancelot;* Rabelais, *Gargantua;* Molière, *Le Misanthrope;* Voltaire, *Candide;* George Sand, *La Mare au diable;* Hugo, *Les Misérables;* Camus, *L'Etranger*).

— can identify at least three major artists and/or musicians, each from a different historical period, and at least one work by each (e.g., Nicolas Poussin, "Les Bergers d'Arcadie"; Claude Debussy, "Prélude à l'après-midi d'un faune"; Marie Laurencin, "Apollinaire et ses amis").
— can identify several important figures in 20th-century popular culture (e.g., Michel Sardou, Patricia Kaas, Eddie Mitchell, François Truffaut, Tintin, Astérix).

Upon completing STAGE 3, the learner:

Communication in Cultural Context
— can express attitudes towards people taking into account social context (e.g., giving and receiving compliments, showing gratitude, apologizing, expressing anger or impatience).
— has some knowledge of regional variations in the target language (e.g., pronunciation in the Midi).
— can interpret some common French gestures not used in American culture (e.g., shrugging of the shoulders to express indifference, pursing of the lips to express doubt).
— can establish and maintain appropriate distance in conversations with French people.
— can understand cryptic references to higher levels of social organization (unions, educational institutions, political parties) and make appropriate inferences (e.g., C.F.D.T, H.E.C., R.P.R.).

The Value System
— can describe six or more highest common values and mental habits in the values context. (See Inventory at the end of this section.)
— can recognize manifestations of the value system when they occur as themes or behaviors in written texts, films, or real life (e.g., the importance of **friendship** as expressed in *Le Petit Prince;* the pride in **resourcefulness** exhibited in the 1970s slogan, "En France on n'a pas de pétrole, mais on a des idées").
— can describe several major differences between French and American values.

Social Patterns and Conventions
— can describe the major recreational and leisure activities (e.g., sports, cinema, television, gardening).
— can discuss similarities and differences between French and American child rearing practices (e.g., attitude toward upbringing, kinds of discipline, activities with their parents, attitude toward schoolwork).
— can discuss important events in the women's rights movement in France (e.g., acquisition of the right to vote in 1944 and the right to have their own bank accounts in 1965, the creation of "Planning familial" centers and abortion legislation in the 1970s).
— can describe changes in the roles of men and women in the family and workplace (e.g., fathers taking care of children, working women with young children).
— is aware of the distinction between practicing and non-practicing Catholics in France.

Social Institutions
— can describe the French administrative and governmental structure (e.g., "Etat, régions, départements, communes, le président de la République, le premier ministre, le gouvernement, l'Assemblée Nationale, le Sénat").

- can identify the principal political parties and their orientations (e.g., "RPR, UDF, Parti socialiste, Parti communiste, Front National, partis écologistes").
- can describe the tension between elitist and egalitarian tendencies in the secondary and higher educational systems and compare them to the American system (e.g., "lycées d'enseignement général" vs. "lycées professionnels," importance of the "Bac scientifique", "Grandes Ecoles" vs. universities).
- can identify the major labor and professional unions and their political orientation (e.g., CGT, CFDT, CGT-FO, FEN, CNPF).
- can describe the main religious groups in France (e.g., Catholics, Moslems, Protestants, Jews).
- can describe some of the social benefits offered by the "Sécurité sociale," and other state agencies (e.g., medical insurance, unemployment compensation, retirement benefits, "allocations familiales").
- can describe current issues related to immigration (e.g., immigrants' right to vote in local elections, building of mosques in France, girls wearing the Moslem scarf at school, naturalization, polygamy).
- can describe the major communication media (e.g., radio and TV channels, Minitel, major newspapers and magazines).
- can name some major scientific and technological achievements and (where possible) the personalities linked to them (e.g., Pasteur and bacteriology, Marie Curie and radioactivity, Professor Luc Montagnier and AIDS research, Concorde, Ariane).
- can describe the major objectives and programs of the European Union (e.g., student exchange programs through ERASMUS, concerted agricultural policy through the PAC, the provisions of the "traité de Maastricht").

Geography and the Environment
- can describe distinctive characteristics of at least six French geographical regions (e.g., general topography, climate, natural resources, economic development).
- can discuss the concerns of the ecologist movement (e.g., nuclear power, recycling, "espaces verts").

History
- can describe the characteristics of the major periods of French history (e.g., assimilation of the Gauls into the Roman Empire, medieval feudal system, growth of the centralized state under the monarchy, Enlightenment stress on reason and human rights, birth of the republican ideal, industrial revolution, the two World Wars, decolonization, the post-'68 period).
- can identify and explain the influence of at least one major figure in each period (e.g., Saint-Louis, Louis XIV, Napoléon, De Gaulle, Simone Veil).
- can explain how colonization led to the creation of French-speaking areas outside Europe (e.g., Quebec, Sub-Saharan Africa, North Africa).

Literature and the Arts
- can describe the work of one major author from each historical period since the Middle Ages and show how the work is representative of each period (e.g., *Les Essais, Le Discours de la méthode, L'Encyclopédie, Madame Bovary, La Nausée*).
- can identify the style of one major painter for each historical period since the Renaissance (e.g., Poussin, La Tour, Watteau, Vigée-Lebrun, Delacroix, Manet, Gauguin, Rouault, Matisse).

— can identify and describe the architectural styles present in five major monuments (e.g., Le Mont-St.-Michel, Chartres or Notre-Dame, Versailles, Chambord, the Opéra Garnier vs. the Opéra de la Bastille, le Palais de Chaillot, the Grande Arche at La Défense).
— can identify some recent outstanding personalities in the areas of film, song, music, journalism, and television and describe briefly their achievements (e.g., the Depardieu phenomenon, Catherine Deneuve, Sophie Marceau, Louis Malle, contemporary French singers, Alain Duhamel, Claire Brétécher, Patrick Poivre d'Arvor, Bernard Pivot, Jacques Chancel).

Upon completing STAGE 4, the learner:

Communication in Cultural Context
— is able to function appropriately in a wide range of social and professional contexts (e.g., social receptions, work-related negotiations).
— can understand and explain humor or irony in a cultural context (e.g., a political cartoon in a newspaper or magazine).
— can use typically French gestures and sounds (e.g., pursing of the lips to express doubt, the expulsion of air expressing rejection or fatigue).
— understands some current physical gestures that accompany or evoke traditional colloquialisms (e.g., "Mon oeil!," "Il est cinglé!," "C'est nul!," etc.).

The Value System
— can discuss the interrelations among the highest common values and mental habits (e.g., the relationship of "individualisme," "méfiance," and "espace privé"; see Inventory at the end of this section).
— can discuss the tensions within the value system (e.g., the conflict between individualism and social conscience).
— can explain the influence of the value system upon some of the major features of French culture (e.g., the centralization and intellectuality characteristic of the school system).

Social Patterns and Conventions
— can write on the main social patterns and conventions in terms of their underlying "themes" and recent trends (e.g., family types in relation to sex roles and the raising of children; social acceptance of single mothers and "union libre"; the effect of the "société des loisirs" on the mentality of people and the economy).

Social Institutions
— can write on recent trends in the main linguistic, economic, political, and educational institutions of France in terms of their underlying "themes" and recent trends (e.g., importance of the French language and reactions to the borrowing of foreign words; the economy in relation to government centralization and to the European Union).
— can describe and explain the stance of the principal political parties on several contemporary issues (e.g., the opposing attitudes of the Socialist party and the "Front National" toward immigrants; the reform of the education system as seen by the left and the right).

Geography and the Environment
— can discuss the development of regional economies in relation to concern for the environment (e.g., nuclear energy, decentralization of industry, tourism).
— can discuss the evolution of the ecologist movement (e.g., from environmental concern to political parties).

History
— can describe long-term trends and patterns in the political, social, and economic history of France (e.g., rise of the middle class, acceptance of parliamentary democracy, educational reforms of the Third Republic).
— can describe the impact on contemporary life of some major historical trends and events (e.g., the creation of the *départements* under the Revolution, influence of Napoléon's *Code civil*, separation of Church and State, the improvements in workers' rights initiated by the Front populaire; the *exode rural* and the gradual shifting of emphasis from the primary, to the secondary, and now to the tertiary sectors of the economy).

Literature and the Arts
— can describe the artistic styles and schools from various periods (e.g., Rococo, Romanticism, Impressionism).
— can describe some 20th-century avant-garde movements in art, drama, music, and literature (e.g., Cubism, Dadaism, Surrealism, the "Nouveau Roman," the Theater of the Absurd, the "Nouvelle Vague" in cinema, Pierre Boulez and computer-generated music).
— demonstrates some knowledge of the contributions of French-speaking Belgium or Switzerland to literature, the arts, and popular culture (e.g., J.-J. Rousseau, Giacometti, Jacques Tinguerly, Michel de Ghelderode, Georges Simenon, Jacques Brel, Hergé).

 # AN INVENTORY OF THE FRENCH VALUE SYSTEM

by Howard L. Nostrand and Claudette Imberton-Hunt

The values we are concerned with here are a dozen or so "highest common values" of French culture, that is, the set of widely-shared fundamental values which are considered to be good and desirable in themselves, and not just a means toward a higher end. The "value system," as conceived here, includes both this set of values and the closely related thought patterns and prevalent assumptions (inventoried below under B) which constitute their context. Together they underlie French behavior, customs, and social institutions and guarantee the coherence of French culture. A knowledge of the value system is thus extremely useful in understanding the phenomena which constitute this culture. Moreover, a particularly productive learning experience consists in relating the surface manifestations of French culture—as they arise in teaching the language, literature, arts, behavior patterns, customs, conventions, and institutions—to the relatively constant themes formed by the culture's value system.

In the course of decades, the relative constants of a culture evolve in response to new conditions. French militarism of earlier centuries, for instance, has lost its glory and ceased to be a common value, while the concern for the environment is adding a new value, "écologisme." Current research (see Appendix II) shows additional changes, although more in cosmopolitan milieux than in "la France profonde." Among these, individualism and the art of living have changed as the rise of informal relationships and social groups provides new opportunities for self-fulfillment, while another value, intellectuality, is tempered by a relaxed acceptance and cultivation of emotion. Yet, all the modifications and the powerful influences of foreign cultures are absorbed into a persistent French identity.

All the elements in the value system interact and sometimes limit one another, as in the opposition between romantic love and realism. There is, moreover, no fixed hierarchy among the values presented here, and it should be emphasized that French culture is particularly rich in contradictions. The great majority of the French decide in each problem situation which of the conflicting values should be given priority.

The evolving system requires an evolving description, which is now facilitated by six main databases. These six, along with nearly a hundred others covering the whole Francophone world, have been identified by H.L. Nostrand and G.R. Upp in *Databases: Our Next Technical Revolution* (Champaign, IL: American Association of Teachers of French, 1991).

A. HIGHEST COMMON VALUES

Friendship / "l'Amitié": A serious relationship reserved for the closest of acquaintances. While Americans tend to make friends easily, the French are slow to grant their full confidence and share their personal life. Forming friendships is a demanding and lengthy process, achieved by stages. Once achieved, it implies a long-term commitment, often for life.

Love / "l'Amour": A sentiment varying from "tendresse" and benevolence to the close ties of parental and conjugal love, and from romantic love to the extreme of passion. Except in this last case, what the French expect of love is limited by their realism. The different facets of love have been a subject of assiduous analysis in French literature since the Middle Ages.

Individualism-Freedom / "l'Individualisme-la Liberté": Two sides of the same value, seen from the standpoint of the individual or from that of a society designed to favor individual self-fulfillment. A strong attachment to independence of mind and conscience, and to non-conformism, leads to a strong resistance against constraints, particularly those imposed by civil authorities or by one's superior in the workplace. French individualism is essentially defensive, in contrast with American individualism.

In opinion polls the French continue to see themselves as individualists, and since the 1980s have even become more so toward formal power, questioning whether politicians, traditionally called "les responsables," can be trusted to solve the deepening problems of society. But meanwhile a tendency toward affiliation has spread (see below), limiting individualism.

Affiliation / "l'Appartenance": A rising value of association in informal groups for current shared purposes. Since the events of May 1968, unofficial groups have become increasingly common in the community, in sports, in street demonstrations separate from the institutionalized unions, and in the workplace, where 85% of the work force are salaried employees who benefit by teamwork and who distrust the top 5% of individualistic managers as being outdated. The elite young graduates of the Ecole Nationale d'Administration, for whom there are no longer enough top positions, see themselves less admired and feared than their predecessors. They feel, and are felt to be, closer to the rest of the people, in a social structure that has become less hierarchical.

Informality / "l'Informalité": In interpersonal relations, a relaxing of the social hierarchy and the expected formalities which had limited the ideal of unpretentiousness. (It has always been praiseworthy for a person entitled to deference to be unassuming, "tout à fait simple.") In the 1990s, informality moves to the center of the value which sanctions individual innovation in the social structure. The rule-circumventing resourcefulness, "la débrouillardise," which served as its center in the 1950s, remains a pattern of thought (see section B below).

The Art of Living / "l'Art de vivre": First of all, the appreciation of pleasures such as good food and conversation. Leisure time is highly valued: French labor unions have negotiated for longer and longer vacations, while American unions have given priority to wages. Secondly, an esthetic concern for taste, an ideal of style. One's clothes are a composition. So is the presentation of food on the table. Conversation, decorum, gestures, all reflect this ideal.

Musical performance, dance, etc., aim to express elegance rather than emotional intensity; sentimentality and exaggeration are looked down on. Third, social know-how, "le savoir-vivre," in a relatively hierarchical society prescribes the consideration corresponding to the social position of one's interlocutor. The new informality is not everywhere acceptable, particularly from an outsider.

Realism / "le Réalisme": A strong will to see objectively and to have no illusions about oneself, the abilities of one's children, and the faults of one's countrymen. Realism sets limits to intellectual conjecturing as well as to expectations. It includes the acceptance of discomfort and unpleasantness as a part of life: "Que voulez-vous?" ("What do you expect?"). It also leads to a matter-of-fact attitude toward the body and its functions, and sometimes to a ribaldry (ascribed to the ancestral Gauls) which can shock the outsider.

Intellectuality / "l'Intellectualité": An ideal which centers upon the capacity to analyze methodically and rigorously, the ability to marshall ideas in a logical sequence and to synthesize them, and an aptitude for elegant organization and expression of the products of the mind. In everyday life, the French value the quality of "lucidity" and the ability to reason. The cultivation of these qualities colors their individualism and realism. Rationality is the pride of the French, and the admonition "Be reasonable" takes on for French children a resonance it does not possess at all in English. This whole ideal is carried out by the thought patterns described below in section B. A contrary value—Emotion—has arisen, however, to limit its domain.

Emotion / "l'Emotion": The progressive acceptance and cultivation of emotion, a major change which began in the 1970s. Among the French under the age of 40, this value has gained ground over the ideal of dispassionate, rational intellectuality which had tended to be uppermost, in reaction against the excesses of Romanticism in the first decades of the nineteenth century. Emotion has come to be regarded not as a weakness but as a proof of vitality.

"La France": A strong attachment to this concept, which includes a deep conviction of the superiority of French civilization, inherited from centuries of cultural dominance. The concept ranges from severely critical appreciation to blatant chauvinism. While a distinction is made between the idealized France and the State, government is not considered an antagonist of the business world, as it tends to be seen by Americans.

Nationalism is being modified by a certain Europeanism. European unity is important as a forward-looking economic and political goal, but it cannot replace the national traditions, at least for some decades ahead, to satisfy the need of individuals for a cultural identity. The European past provides no shared object of loyalty capable of producing the symbolic rallying point for a sense of European cultural identity. Identification with Europe increases during young adulthood, however, in France as in other European countries. To the question, "In the near future, do you see yourself as just French, French and European, European and French, or just European?", 1,000 responses divided by age groups as follows: 15-year-olds (49.3% French, **41.7%** French and European, 3.4% European and French, 3.1% European only); cf. 16 to 19-year-olds (29.5%, **57%**, 6.1%, 5%) and 20-year-olds and above (17.1%, **64%**, 8.5%, 8.4%). Source: Enquête Université de Nantes-Eurobaromètre, Spring, 1992 (see *Evaluation d'une action pour la Dimension Européenne dans l'Education,* p. 119). The poll shows similar results for five other European countries. See Bibliography E.3.

The remaining highest common values ("justice," "fraternité") are equally important, since all elements of the system interact, but they require less attention because they so closely resemble their counterparts in the American value system. "Justice" is two separate values. The concern for *social* justice is a legacy, in the French context, of the Revolution's ideal of "Egalité," which includes a steady advance in this century toward equality of the sexes. Entirely different is *criminal* justice, which protects personal security. The concern for "Fraternité" inherited from the Revolution appears, for example, in the national program of health insurance, and it has expanded to mean a universal humanitarian spirit exemplified by associations such as Médecins sans Frontières. Related to this spirit is the growing concern for the environment.

B. THE CONTEXT OF THE VALUES

The elements of the social-psychological infrastructure which interact with the values to give them a meaning specific to French culture are of two types. Thought patterns shape the *process* of thinking, while the assumptions about human nature and society act as cultural *content*.

1. Characteristic Thought Patterns

Logical Reasoning / "l'Esprit cartésien": The taste for reasoning, reinforced by a tendency to analyze things, situations, and people with an independent mind, and by a penchant for manipulating abstract ideas. Americans, on the contrary, distrust abstractions and seize upon the example or the precedent, in public discussion as in the legal system. This pattern of reasoning carries out the value of intellectuality (rationality being both an aspect of that value, in the sense that it is a subject of pride, and a thought pattern, in the sense that it is a way of conducting one's thought).

Distrust / "la Méfiance": An habitual skepticism toward the unknown or untried—whether situations or persons—which contrasts with the American confidence in progress and human goodness. The distrust of outsiders ("les autres") explains in part why the French do not bestow their friendship readily, and why they react with reserve to any overture that may seem aggressive. This thought pattern is supported by the presupposition that appearances may be deceptive.

Resourcefulness / "la Débrouillardise": Pride in ingenuity, particularly when one achieves one's ends despite official constraints and obstacles. "Le système D," as they ironically call this rule-circumventing non-system, is considered a sign of intelligence and independence of mind. The pattern remains important, for example in connection with the defensive attitude toward taxes (an attitude which goes back to the arbitrary taxation under the monarchy). But the rising values of affiliation and informality (see above, section A) have taken on greater importance in the adaptation of the individual to society.

Contextual Thinking and Systems Analysis / "le Relationnisme et la Systémique": Basically, a centuries-old French concern to take the context into account as an integral part of defining a thing, a situation, or a person. Americans tend on the contrary to see the object alone, independent of attachments. Moreover, the French prefer a well-delimited context, for example in their closed form of enumeration from A to C "en passant par B," while Anglophones assume an open-ended series, "A,B,C" (see H. Nostrand, "French Culture's Concern for Relationships," in Bibliography B).

By the 1990s a more developed form of relationism, essentially the approach called systems analysis, has spread through the French population. The expectation of a simple cause and effect is yielding to the comprehension that the real world consists of interdependent parts, and a consequent distrust of the simple solution, "Y a qu'à" ("All you have to do is . . .").

The Tendency to Categorize / "le Compartimentage": A dislike of mixing objects of different categories, like "sucré" and "salé" in cooking, or work and vacation. Private, interior space is clearly distinguished from exterior space. It is in fact characteristic of high-context cultures, as defined by Edward T. Hall, to have preestablished categories in which one inserts new objects (see, for example, his *Hidden Differences* or *Beyond Culture* in Bibliography B). This cognitive pattern is related to those of rationality and contextual thinking, as well as to the value of intellectuality.

Centralization / "la Centralisation": The penchant for organizing a conceptual whole around a center. This tendency recurs in the concentration of administrative and economic power in Paris, in the fact that distances within France are measured from a point in front of Notre Dame Cathedral, in the radial pattern of the railroads and highways—and in the idea of the radiating diffusion of French civilization.

2. Prevalent Assumptions

Appearances are Deceptive: The suspicion that the appearance of a thing, a situation, or a person may not correspond to the inner reality. This presupposition underlies the habit of distrust and contributes to the importance of intellectuality, for it is the role of intellect to penetrate the deceptive surface.

The Primacy of the Individual and of Individual Interests over Those of Society: This assumption, basic to individualism, is the opposite of the assumption underlying communitarian cultures. It is expected, however, that the individual will contribute toward a society capable of promoting the self-fulfillment of its members.

Space is Limited and Categorized: The French are accustomed to limited space, both interior and exterior. The vast expanses of the American West seem exotic. Secondly, private space is sharply distinguished, as a rule, from public space. A front gate is kept closed, as is the door of an office, a bedroom, or a bathroom. After dark, the shutters are closed. An intermediate category is required, however, for back alleys, outdoor markets, and other exceptions, which form an intervening continuum between private and completely public space.

Time is Categorized, and Managed "Polychronically": Leisure time is sharply demarcated from work time. The management of time is "polychronic" rather than "monochronic": unlike the "one-track mind," one pursues a number of different objectives concurrently (see Edward T.

Hall's works referred to above). Americans, relatively less preoccupied by the context and possible side effects of an action, have a stronger tendency to concentrate their attention on one thing at a time in order to reach an objective—"to get the job done."

 FRENCH-SPEAKING NORTH AMERICA

Coordinator: Paul Barrette, University of Tennessee

There are several well-established communities of French speakers in North America, most of whom trace their origins back to the original French settlements in the Bay of Fundy and the St. Lawrence valley during the seventeenth century. By far the largest and most important of the North American French-speaking societies is in Quebec. Its seven million French speakers, with important cultural and economic centers in Montreal and Quebec City, form the nucleus of French society in Canada. Most of the indicators in this section will focus on Quebec culture. About a million more French speakers continue their linguistic heritage in other provinces of Canada, primarily eastern Ontario, St. Boniface in Manitoba, in northern and eastern New Brunswick, and in parts of Nova Scotia. The descendants of nineteenth-century French immigrants to New England still flourish (around 2.3 million) and maintain islands of French culture in that part of the United States. In Louisiana, where over a million people claim French origin, French is still spoken by a small Creole community dating from the French settlement of New Orleans, and a larger "Cajun" group of speakers who descend from the survivors of the British expulsion of French speakers from Acadia (the Bay of Fundy) in 1755. Together, these communities constitute a significant part of the French-speaking world.

INDICATORS OF COMPETENCE

Upon completing STAGE 1, the learner:

Communication in Cultural Context
— knows that some French-speaking Canadians use "Bonjour" and "Comment ça va?" to say "Hello," while sometimes using "Bonjour" for "Goodby" also.
— knows that the familiar/formal distinction between "tu" and "vous" used in Europe is maintained, but that many North American speakers use "tu" as the general singular without connotations of familiarity.
— knows that the "tu" forms are more prevalent at higher levels in the social hierarchy than in Europe.

The Value System
Competence in this category begins at Stage 2.

Social Patterns and Conventions
— knows that the daily schedule (meal times, office hours) is more closely aligned with the American than with the continental French model.
— knows several traditional or regional dishes (e.g., "soupe aux pois" and "poutine" in Quebec, "tourtière" and "cretons" in Quebec and New England, and "jambalaya" and "gumbo" in Louisiana).
— knows that French, English, and American cuisine are all present in French-speaking Canada (e.g., crêpes, roast beef, and hamburgers all appear on restaurant menus) and that a great variety of additional national cuisines can be enjoyed in the metropolitan centers.
— is aware of the importance of winter sports in French-speaking Canada, especially ice hockey (e.g., can name an important French-Canadian hockey team and its home city).

Social Institutions
— can identify the Canadian and Quebec flags and knows their symbolic meanings.
— can recognize Canadian currency (coins and banknotes).

Geography and the Environment
— knows that Quebec is a province of Canada and can locate it on a map of North America.
— knows the general size of the French-Speaking population in Canada (e.g., French-speakers represent around a quarter of the population of Canada and around 80% of the residents of the province of Quebec).
— can identify the principal French-Speaking areas in the United States (e.g., New England, Louisiana).
— can identify any French-speaking communities in the student's own state.

History
— can identify some of the first French explorers, settlers, and missionaries in the New World (e.g., Cartier, Champlain, Du Gua de Monts, Marquette, Joliet, La Salle, La Hontan, Charlevoix, Jesuit fathers and Ursuline sisters, etc.).

Literature and the Arts
— knows a few simple folk and contemporary songs and/or poems (e.g., "A la claire fontaine," "O Canada," Gilles Vigneault's "Gens du pays").

Upon completing STAGE 2, the learner:

Communication in Cultural Context
— can identify some typical Franco-Canadian expressions and grammatical structures (e.g., the use of "Bienvenue!" for "You're welcome!" and "tanné" for "fatigué"; less frequently, the use of "piastre" for "dollar" and "char" for "voiture").

— can identify some typical Franco-Canadian pronunciations (e.g., use of "mwé" and "twé" for "moi" and "toi"; replacing "elle" with "a" and "ils" with "i" in colloquial speech; use of "ts" and "dz" before the front vowels "i" and "u," as in "tu" pronounced "tsu"; use of the rolled "r" and of a high nasal sound where continental French has lowered it, as in "vent," "prend," and "-ment" almost rhyming with "vin").

— is aware of the sensitivity concerning the use of French or English in Quebec.

The Value System

— knows the motto "Je me souviens" (on all licence plates) and understands the historical reference (the defeat on the Plains of Abraham) and the implicit attachment to the French heritage.

— knows the French speakers' historical attachment to the land and to the Catholic church, as well as the attenuation of these traits today.

— knows the French speakers' ambivalent attitudes toward France, Great Britain, and the federal government of Canada.

Social Patterns and Conventions

— knows the historical and literary importance of oral tale-telling and humorous oral anecdotes in Quebec culture.

— knows the "rang" system of land distribution and its importance to social life in rural Quebec.

Social Institutions

— knows the current ruling party in Quebec and can name the province's current prime minister.

— knows that Quebec is governed in part by an "Assemblée Nationale."

— knows the current major political and social issues and figures (e.g., Bouchard and the "Bloc québécois", Parizeau and the Parti Québécois, Chrétien and federalism).

Geography and the Environment

— is able to identify on a map of North America the most important Francophone areas of Canada outside of Quebec (e.g., regions of New Brunswick, Ontario, Manitoba, Saskatchewan, and Alberta).

— knows basic facts about the geography and climate of French-speaking areas of North America (e.g., St. Lawrence valley, the eastern townships, the harsh northern climate, James Bay).

History

— can relate the "conquest" of New France by the British in the 18th century.

— can relate the expulsion of the Acadians by the English, their eventual settlement in Louisiana, and the development of two different "French" groups in Louisiana: Creoles and Cajuns.

— can relate the migration of great numbers of inhabitants of Quebec to New England in the 19th and early 20th centuries.

Literature and the Arts

— can identify some artists and give examples of artistic expression (from music, film, poetry, theater, or short stories) in Quebec and in other parts of North America (e.g., Michel Tremblay, Louis Fréchette, Emile Nelligan, Louis Dantin, Jacques Ferron, Roch Carrier, Roger Lemelin (les Plouffe), Robert Charlebois, Beausoleil).

Upon completing STAGE 3, the learner:

Communication in Cultural Context
— can describe additional major differences between French and French-Canadian pronunciations (e.g., diphthongization of many vowels, pronunciation of "i, u, ou" with less tension before a consonant, the maintenance of two distinct "a" sounds).
— can identify some differences between the grammar of French and French-Canadian, such as gender of nouns, use of pronouns, interrogatives (e.g., "un offre," "lui aider," "va-t'en pas"), while being aware that these forms are heard less and less frequently today.
— can recognize origins of lexical differences between French and French-Canadian (e.g., anglicisms, archaisms, adaptations to local needs).
— understands how and why the debate took place over the status of "joual" and is aware of the diminished importance of that debate in Quebec today.
— knows that new feminine forms are being used in Quebec (e.g., in the professions: *auteure* and *écrivaine*), which have not yet gained widespread acceptance in France.

The Value System
— can explain the attitudes implicit in expressions such as "les deux solitudes" and "la basse ville" in reference to Montreal (quartier historique) and Quebec City (quartier populaire).
— can explain the cultural implications of terms such as "la revanche des berceaux," "la grande noirceur," "le grand dérangement," "speak white."

Social Patterns and Conventions
— can discuss the ethnic diversity of Montreal and its influence on the Quebec identity (e.g., the powerful English-speaking minority alongside communities of Jews, Italians, Haitians, Arabs, Portuguese, etc.).

Social Institutions
— can describe the relationship between the Quebec government and the Canadian federal government (e.g., the large measure of autonomy accorded Quebec).
— can discuss the role of the church in the political, educational, and social arenas (e.g., control of education by the church until the first half of the 20th century; promotion of traditional attachment to the land—as a promotion of stability—throughout the 19th and first half of the 20th century).

Geography and the Environment
— can demonstrate basic familiarity with the general layouts of urban centers such as Montreal and Quebec City, with their monuments and distinctive features.
— can identify and describe French-speaking areas within New England and Louisiana.

History
— can place chronologically the "Révolution tranquille" and the "FLQ".
— can relate the major changes during the "Révolution tranquille" and their importance.
— can trace and discuss the role of René Lévesque and the Parti Québécois (e.g., the independence movement, the referendum of 1980).
— can describe the issues of the linguistic debate during the 70s and 80s and the significance of "la Loi 101."

Literature and the Arts
— can demonstrate knowledge of major literary figures and their works (e.g., Gabrielle Roy, Anne Hébert, Michel Tremblay, Antonine Maillet, Hubert Aquin, Jacques Godbout, Jacques Poulin, Honoré Beaugrand, Ferdinand Gagnon, Jack Kerouac, etc.).
— is familiar with the music and poetry of Félix Leclerc, Gilles Vigneault, and Zachary Richard, as well as the music of some more recent singers such as Céline Dion.
— can recognize the French influence on the architecture of certain structures (e.g., churches) in New England and Louisiana.

Upon completing STAGE 4, the learner:

Communication in Cultural Context
— demonstrates a broad understanding of oral Québécois French and literary manifestations of oral forms (e.g., Michel Tremblay, Gérald Godin, Gaston Miron).
— exhibits an awareness of levels of language specific to Quebec.

The Value System
— is aware of the extent to which traditional attitudes exist alongside modern outlooks turned towards the future in commerce, culture, and politics.

Social Patterns and Conventions
— has knowledge of present-day immigration and its implications.

Social Institutions
— is able to discuss current Franco-Canadian political concerns in the context of the Canadian Federation.
— is familiar with and can discuss the implications of such recent developments as the Meech Lake accords, the failed referendum on the Charlottetown proposal for constitutional revision, and the narrowly defeated referendum on the independence of Québec (October 1995).

Geography and the Environment
— is aware of the conflict between Indians and other Québécois with respect to the James Bay hydroelectric project.

History
— can explain the importance of figures such as Lord Durham and Louis Riel in the historical consciousness of Canadians and Québécois.
— demonstrates familiarity with the Duplessis regime (pre-1960) and the role of Jean Lesage.
— can explain the "crise d'octobre" (1970) and the subsequent actions of the Trudeau government (e.g., martial law).
— can discuss how the role of Trudeau in recent Canadian history is evaluated differently by different groups (e.g., hostility of many residents of Quebec).

Literature and the Arts
— can demonstrate knowledge of major themes of Quebec literature and of the works where they are found (e.g., the theme of "emigration" in *Maria Chapdelaine, Trente Arpents, Pélagie-la-Charrette,* and *Ces enfants de ma vie;* the theme of "alienation" in *Prochain Episode, Le Temps des hommes,* and *Une Saison dans la vie d'Emmanuel*).

— is acquainted with major film directors and their works (e.g., Claude Jutra, Pierre Perrault, Denys Arcand).

— is aware of the contributions of some earlier North American Francophone writers and musicians (e.g., the frères Rouquette and Alfred Mercier from Louisiana, contributors to Les Cénelles, Calixa Lavallée).

FRENCH-SPEAKING SUB-SAHARAN AFRICA

*Coordinators: Charles Hancock, Ohio State University
Lauren Yoder, Davidson College*

The Black African Francophone cultural community is spread throughout West and Central Africa and includes some island nations, like Madagascar, in the African sphere. French is an official and prestige language of instruction in over twenty Sub-Saharan countries, all former French or Belgian colonies, which include over 14 million speakers of French.

INDICATORS OF COMPETENCE

Upon completing STAGE 1, the learner:

Communication in Cultural Context
— knows the importance of oral communication for Black African speakers of French, particularly as regards greetings and good-byes (oral comments and reactions are typically expected).
— knows that "tu" is used much more widely than in Europe (in most African languages, in fact, the distinction between "tu" and "vous" is nonexistent).
— is aware that greetings typically include questions about the family, and in much of West Africa are influenced greatly by traditional Islamic greetings.

The Value System
— recognizes the importance of hospitality and generosity.
— knows how much personal dignity is valued (e.g., realizes that you do not take pictures without permission).

Social Patterns and Conventions
— is aware of the importance of color, especially vivid colors, in most African dress styles.

Social Institutions
— can identify typical tropical foods (e.g., manioc, mango, papaya) which are part of many Africans' daily lives.

Geography and the Environment
— can identify and locate on a world map the major areas in and around Sub-Saharan Africa where French is spoken (e.g., West Africa, Central Africa, Madagascar).
— is aware of the major climatic conditions and topography of Sub-Saharan Africa (e.g., can distinguish between the arid savannahs of the Sahel and the tropical forests of the West African coast and Central Africa).

History
— knows that there were flourishing civilizations in Africa before the arrival of Europeans.
— understands that millions of Africans were uprooted during at least two centuries of the Atlantic slave trade.
— knows that the French-speaking countries of Sub-Saharan Africa were once either French or Belgian colonies.

Literature and the Arts
— can identify typical musical instruments (e.g., the drum and the marimba) and is aware of the popularity of rhythmic sounds with heavy percussion.
— recognizes the importance of music and dance in traditional African culture.
— is aware of the particular importance of the drum in African music (the word for drum and the word for music are identical in some African languages) and of its symbolic value (e.g., the human heartbeat, cyclical events).

Upon completing STAGE 2, the learner:

Communication in Cultural Context
— is aware that linguistic variation results from interference from different local languages in traditional African settings; i.e., several different pronunciations for a particular sound (e.g., "a" as in *parler*) are acceptable.

The Value System
— recognizes group identity (as opposed to individualism) as a prominent value.
— understands, as a corollary of the above, that self-identity is typically found through group relationships.
— is aware that time is measured experientially with a focus on the past and the present.

Social Patterns and Conventions
— understands how to bargain for simple objects in an open air market.
— is familiar with the role that group membership (e.g., tribal unit, extended family) plays in African life.
— is aware that while some people in Francophone Black Africa maintain traditional life-styles (e.g., herding and artisanal metalworking), many others pursue careers in a wide range of contemporary professions such as teaching, medicine, engineering, and business.

Social Institutions
— is familiar with some local currencies (e.g., the CFA franc, used in most Francophone Black African countries).
— is aware of the prevalence of open-air markets.
— recognizes the ceremonial nature of much social interaction (e.g., the tea ceremony in Islamic West Africa).
— is aware of the presence of Islam, Christianity, and traditional African religions and knows that Islam is much more prevalent in West Africa than in Central Africa.

Geography and the Environment
— is aware of demographic pressures and their effect on the environment in Sub-Saharan Africa.
— can identify and locate on a world map five Francophone countries in Sub-Saharan Africa and their capitals.
— can identify areas where drought is endemic (e.g., the Sahel).

History
— is aware that Africans who speak French natively have developed *both* an African and a European history and can give several examples of the mixture of African roots and European influences (e.g., European-style weddings and polygamy).
— is aware of the movement toward political and cultural independence of the Sub-Saharan French and Belgian colonies in the 50s and 60s.
— can recognize some important figures in recent Francophone Black African history (e.g., Senghor, Sékou Touré, Lumumba, Houphouet-Boigny).

Literature and the Arts
— knows that visual arts are important, with a focus on vivid colors and frequent mixing of geometric forms (e.g., tie-dyes in cloth).
— can recognize the style of traditional wood sculpture.
— is aware of the importance of story telling and of oral literature.
— can identify at least one Black African or Malagasy author (e.g., Camara Laye, Leopold Senghor, Bernard Dadie, Jacques Rabemananjara).

Upon completing STAGE 3, the learner:

Communication in Cultural Context
— is aware that grammar, pronunciation, and word choices of speakers may vary from standard European usage, reflecting a particular historico-cultural context and tradition and/or the influence of different local or European languages (e.g., "elle n'a pas vu rien," modeled on the negative suffix in Wolof, the confusion between "sentir," "écouter," and "entendre" in parts of Zaire due to interference from Lingala, and the English-influenced expression "le bayam-sellam" to indicate a small peddler in Cameroon).

The Value System
— knows the importance of the role of ancestors (as an aspect of the focus on the past).

— knows the importance of the concept of unity (i.e., everything is functionally connected) in traditional African culture.
— is aware that in traditional African settings harmony with nature is valued (e.g., planting and harvest festivals).

Social Patterns and Conventions
— is aware of the essential role of the oral tradition in passing along cultural values and mores (as well as family and group history) to the next generation.
— understands the "extended family" concept, i.e., knows that even distant relations are considered to be important family members (e.g., in African languages, the word for "cousin" is frequently no different from the word "brother" or "sister"), and that each person is thought to be related in some way to all other Africans.
— knows that African cultures include both the traditional extended family concept (i.e., a large number of people living in a single compound) and the more European model of the nuclear family (i.e., only parents and their children living in the same dwelling).
— is aware that often an uncle takes responsibility for a child's education.

Social Institutions
— is aware of the presence of multiple ethnic groups.
— is familiar with elements of different religious practices (e.g., Islam, Christianity, and traditional religion).
— can describe the role of the "griots" and tribal elders in traditional African societies.
— has a basic knowledge of the style of government of at least one Black Francophone African country.
— can describe the economic strengths and weaknesses of the above country.

Geography and the Environment
— can identify and locate on a world map ten Francophone countries in Sub-Saharan Africa and their capitals.
— can identify at least two major rivers in Francophone Africa.
— can name the major crops or primary resources (e.g., coffee, cocoa, copper, timber) of several Francophone countries.

History
— can demonstrate basic knowledge of the colonial and post-colonial history of one Black Francophone African country.
— is familiar with the role of Léopold Senghor as a political and cultural figure in Senegal, as well as his poet laureat status.
— can identify such historico-mythic figures as Soundjata.

Literature and the Arts
— knows that poetry and other symbolic language use is highly valued.
— knows that the drum as a symbol of the human heartbeat occurs in Black African Francophone poetry (as well as in music).

— can describe and explain the "Négritude" movement.
— can name at least one work by each of two Black Francophone African writers (e.g., Camara Laye, *L'Enfant noir;* Mariama Ba, *Une Si Longue Lettre;* Birago Diop, *Les Contes d'Amadou Koumba*).
— can describe the work of one major Francophone African author.
— recognizes the name of at least one African film director (e.g., Sembene Ousmane, Souleymane Cissé, Gaston Kaboré).

Upon completing STAGE 4, the learner:

Communication in Cultural Context
— is aware that French is perceived in Africa as the language of the elite and of social advancement.

The Value System
— can discuss the conflicts engendered by the confrontation of traditional African values and European values.
— can discuss the social and political consequences of the blending of African and European perspectives.

Social Patterns and Conventions
— can explain the relationship between basic values, social patterns, and personal behavior in a Black African Francophone society (e.g., the practice of welcoming even distant relatives into the family circle for extended periods).

Social Institutions
— can discuss the relationship between ethnic groups in at least one African country.
— is familiar with differences between social classes.
— can discuss some current links (political, social, economic) between France and Black Francophone Africa.
— is familiar with the general economic topography of some Black Francophone African countries.
— can describe the political climate in at least one Black Francophone African country with reference to political parties and leadership styles.
— can describe some differences between West Africa, Central Africa, and Madagascar.

Geography and the Environment
— can identify the majority of the Francophone countries and their capitals in Sub-Saharan Africa.
— understands how the present national boundaries were set and the pressures both to change and preserve them.

History
— knows the period and relative order of accession to independence of former French and Belgian colonies in Sub-Saharan Africa.

— can name at least three current leaders of Black Francophone African countries and the countries they represent.
— understands the place and influence of Black Francophone African nations in international organizations such as the United Nations and the World Bank.

Literature and the Arts
— can identify several West and Central Francophone African authors and their works, in addition to those identified earlier.
— can show how the work of one major Black Francophone African author relates to the work of other Francophone African authors.
— can discuss, in the context of specific works, some of the major themes of Black Francophone African literature and compare them across cultures (e.g., cyclical time, relationship to the earth, family ties, conflict of cultures).
— can describe the role of the visual arts in some Black Francophone African societies.
— can discuss several films by Black Francophone African filmmakers.

 THE FRENCH-SPEAKING CARIBBEAN

Coordinators: Charles Hancock, Ohio State University
Lauren Yoder, Davidson College

The Francophone cultural community is a strong presence in the Caribbean. French is an official and prestige language of instruction in Haiti, where Francophones comprise 15 to 20% of the population, as well as in Martinique, Guadeloupe, and La Guyane. The latter three, many of whose inhabitants speak both French and Creole, have been overseas departments of the French Republic (Départements d'Outre-Mer or D.O.M.) since 1946.

Francophone Africa and the Caribbean share a common history—uprooting due to slavery, colonialism—and common values such as respect for ancestors and the acceptance of a spirit world. However, specific social, cultural, and political realities of Africa and the Caribbean vary widely, and other traditions (Asian and Amerindian in addition to European) have helped create a distinctly Caribbean identity. Accordingly, the indicators of proficiency in the culture of the French Caribbean are presented separately in this section.

INDICATORS OF COMPETENCE

Upon completing STAGE 1, the learner:

Communication in Cultural Context
— knows the importance of oral communication for Caribbean speakers of French, particularly as regards greetings and good-byes (oral comments and reactions are typically expected).
— knows that "tu" is used much more widely in the Caribbean than in Europe.
— is aware of the co-existence of Creole with French in the Caribbean and that the primary language of most Haitians is Creole.

The Value System
— recognizes the importance of hospitality and generosity.
— knows how much personal dignity is valued (e.g., realizes that you do not take pictures without permission).

Social Patterns and Conventions
— is aware of the importance of color, especially vivid colors, in most Caribbean dress styles.

Social Institutions
— can identify typical tropical foods (e.g., manioc, breadfruit, mango, papaya) which are part of many Caribbean peoples' daily lives.

Geography and the Environment
— can identify and locate on a world map the Caribbean areas where French is spoken by people of African heritage (e.g., Haiti, Martinique, Guadeloupe, La Guyane).
— is aware of the critical relationship between the French Caribbean communities and the sea (e.g., the historical vulnerability to devastating hurricanes).

History
— knows that Amerindian societies existed in the Caribbean before the arrival of the Europeans and Africans.
— is aware that Caribbean society was built around slavery.
— knows that Martinique, Guadeloupe, and La Guyane, former French colonies, are now departments of France.
— knows that Haiti has been independent since the beginning of the 19th century (1804).

Literature and the Arts
— can identify typical musical instruments (eg., drums such as the *gros-ka*) and is aware of the popularity of rhythmic sounds with heavy percussion in Caribbean cultures.
— is aware of the popularity of Creole music (e.g., zouk) and of dancing.

Upon completing STAGE 2, the learner:

Communication in Cultural Context
— is aware that the interplay between French and Creole in traditional Caribbean settings produces variations from European norms in pronunciation and vocabulary.

The Value System
— recognizes group identity (as opposed to individualism) as a prominent value in Caribbean cultures.
— understands, as a corollary of the above, that self identity is typically found through group relationships.

Social Patterns and Conventions
— understands how to bargain for simple objects in an open air market.
— is familiar with the role that group membership (e.g., extended family) plays in the life of the Caribbean speaker of French.
— is aware that while some people maintain traditional life-styles (e.g., fishing), many others pursue careers in a wide range of contemporary professions such as teaching, medicine, engineering, and business.

- understands that life in the French Caribbean is organized much as it is in France, but that rural villages in Haiti are more African in appearance.
- knows that the life-style of predominantly rural Haiti is largely defined by subsistence farming.

Social Institutions
- is familiar with some local currencies (e.g., the French franc used in Martinique and the other French departments in the Caribbean, the *gourde* used in Haiti).
- is aware of the prevalence of open-air markets.
- is aware of the dominance of the Catholic church in the French Caribbean and the coexistence of catholicism, protestantism, and voodoo in Haiti.
- is aware of the traditional dominance of the sugar-cane plantations and their effect on individual lives (e.g., the cyclical nature of employment, the role of the company store).

Geography and the Environment
- can identify and locate on a world map the three French departments and Haiti.
- understands the volcanic origin of the islands and the presence of active volcanoes on some islands.
- recognizes the commercial and symbolic value of the sea to the French Caribbean (e.g., fishing and shipping, but also evokes deadly tropical storms as well as the memory of incoming slaves).

History
- knows that slavery was permanently abolished in Haiti at the beginning of the nineteenth century and in the rest of the French Caribbean by the middle of the century.
- can recognize some important figures in Caribbean history (e.g., Toussaint L'Ouverture, Victor Schoelcher, Aimé Césaire).
- knows that Martinique, Guadeloupe, and La Guyane became French departments shortly after the end of World War II (1946).

Literature and the Arts
- can recognize the style of traditional Haitian wood sculpture.
- is aware of the importance of story telling, folklore, and oral literature.
- can identify at least one author from the French Caribbean (e.g., Roumain, Condé, Juminer, Glissant).

Upon completing STAGE 3, the learner:

Communication in Cultural Context
- can provide examples of variations in grammar, pronunciation, and word choices of French Caribbean speakers in relation to standard European usage, reflecting a particular historico-cultural context and tradition and/or the influence of Creole (e.g., use of the expression "les habitants" to indicate crayfish in Guadeloupe and Martinique).

The Value System
- knows the importance of the role of ancestors (as an aspect of the focus on the past).

Social Patterns and Conventions
— is aware of the essential role of the oral tradition in passing cultural values and mores (as well as family and group history) along to the next generation.

Social Institutions
— is aware of the presence of multiple ethnic groups in the French Caribbean (e.g., Asian, African, and European).
— is familiar with elements of different religious practices (e.g., voodoo).
— is aware of the tensions and mutual interests characterizing the relations between the local whites ("békés"), French people who are not permanent residents, and the majority African-Caribbean population in the French departments.
— is aware of the tensions and mutual interests characterizing the relations between the Francophone and Creolophone populations of Haiti.
— is aware of the links and tensions between Christianity and voodoo in Haiti.

Geography and the Environment
— can locate on a map several important cities in the French Caribbean (e.g., Port-au-Prince, Fort-de-France, Pointe-à-Pitre, Cap Haïtien).
— understands the relationship between eroded mountains, dense population, and out-migration from Haiti.
— can name major crops or primary resources (e.g., bananas, sugar) in the French Caribbean.

History
— can demonstrate basic knowledge of slave rebellions in the Francophone Caribbean and of the events leading to Haitian independence (including, in particular, the roles of Toussaint L'Ouverture and Dessalines).
— is aware of the constant conflict between France and other European powers in the Caribbean over the centuries.
— understands the role of the maroon in Caribbean history.
— is aware of the tensions and links between the United States and Haiti.

Literature and the Arts
— knows that poetry and other symbolic language use is highly valued in French Caribbean cultures.
— knows that the drum as a symbol of the human heartbeat occurs in Francophone poetry (as well as in music) in the Caribbean.
— can describe and explain the "Négritude" movement.
— can name at least one work by each of two Caribbean writers (e.g., Maryse Condé, *Moi, Tituba sorcière;* Aimé Césaire, *La Tragédie du roi Christophe;* Jacques Roumain, *Gouverneurs de la rosée;* Edouard Glissant, *La Lézarde*).
— can describe the work of one major French Caribbean author.
— recognizes and can discuss the importance of Haitian art in the 20th century (e.g., works by Wilson Bigaud, Préfète Duffaut, Rigaud Benoit).
— is aware that the conch shell is widely used as a symbol for maroons in French Caribbean art and literature.

Upon completing STAGE 4, the learner:

Communication in Cultural Context
— is aware that French is perceived in the Caribbean as the language of the elite and of social advancement.
— is aware that the use of Creole is frequently identified, on a symbolic level, with support for cultural or political independence in both Haiti and the French Caribbean.

The Value System
— can discuss the different elements which combine to form the Caribbean identity (e.g., ethnic mix, links to the sea, relationship to metropolitan France).

Social Patterns and Conventions
— can explain the relationship between basic values, social patterns, and personal behavior in French Caribbean societies. (e.g., the importance of group identity as expressed in the concept of the *lakou* in Haiti, the immediate neighborhood which is the locus for voodoo temple and other commercial and communal activities).

Social Institutions
— can discuss the relationship between ethnic groups in at least one area of the Caribbean.
— is familiar with differences between social classes.
— can discuss some current links (political, social, economic) between France and the French Caribbean.
— is familiar with the general economic topography of the French Caribbean.
— can outline the different political tendencies in the French Caribbean (e.g., the movements for autonomy, independence, or full integration).
— can describe the opposing elements on the Haitian political landscape.
— can discuss the relationship between Haitians in Haiti and Haitians living in Canada or the United States.
— can describe the influence and integration of East Asian populations in the French Caribbean.

Geography and the Environment
— can discuss the influence of Hispanophone and Anglophone neighbors in the Western Hemisphere on the economy and society of the French Caribbean (e.g., connections between Cuban *santeria*, Brazilian *macoumba*, and Haitian voodoo).

History
— can trace the development of the current political and social situation from a plantation colonial economy to the present day.
— is aware of the role of the French Caribbean in world events, such as during World War II.
— is able to discuss the current value to France of association with the French Caribbean.
— can describe historical and contemporary links between Haiti and the French Caribbean.

Literature and the Arts
— can show how the work of one major Caribbean author relates to the work of other Caribbean authors.
— can discuss some of the major themes of Caribbean literature (e.g., the nature of the relationship with Africa, the role of the sea, the transmission of culture, the cane fields, the development of a unique Caribbean identity).
— can outline the interrelationship between continental France and the French Caribbean.
— can perceive differences between literary concerns of Haitian writers and of the French overseas departments.

FRENCH-SPEAKING NORTH AFRICA

Coordinator: Jawed Zouari, Seattle Central College

The French-speaking countries of North Africa (Morocco, Algeria, and Tunisia), all former colonies or protectorates of France, are important for their contribution to French literature and for their current impact on the demography of France. They are also of particular interest to American education as the meeting ground between the West and the Middle-East, whose confrontation produces a sometimes perplexing conflict of values and mores, as well as political and religious institutions.

INDICATORS OF COMPETENCE

Upon completing STAGE 1, the learner:

Communication in Cultural Context
— is aware that while French is widely spoken in North Africa it is identified with colonial history.

The Value System
Competence in this category begins at Stage 2.

Social Patterns and Conventions
— is aware of the importance of deference to elders in Maghrebi society.
— is aware of the tradition of formality toward women (e.g., avoidance of direct eye contact and use of potentially embarrassing language).
— is aware of and understands the reasons for the general separation of the sexes.
— can identify some national dishes (e.g., couscous, tajine, brochettes).

Social Institutions
— is aware that the dominant (and official) religion in North Africa is Islam and that the Moslem houses of worship are mosques.
— knows that alcoholic beverages are forbidden by the Islamic religion.

Geography and the Environment
— can identify Morocco, Algeria, and Tunisia on a world map.
— is aware of their geographical proximity to France.

History
— knows that Morocco, Algeria, and Tunisia are former French colonies or protectorates.

Literature and the Arts
— can recognize the typical architectural style of mosques.

Upon completing STAGE 2, the learner:

Communication in Cultural Context
— understands that loud conversations both in private and in public are typical expressions of the passionate interaction between friends and relatives.

The Value System
— knows that generosity, as shown by warmth and hospitality toward friends as well as strangers, is a particularly valued trait in Maghrebi societies.

Social Patterns and Conventions
— knows that the Maghrebi culture is an amalgam of Arabo-Islamic, Berber, and Mediterranean traditions.
— recognizes the difference between the educated and the non-educated members of the Maghrebi population.
— understands the ambiguity of the Maghrebi identity oscillating between Arab authenticity and mimicry of French life-styles.

Social Institutions
— is familiar with the currencies of the three countries.
— can identify the current Heads of State (Prime Ministers) of Algeria and Tunisia, and the King of Morocco.

Geography and the Environment
— can identify the capitals and other major cities in each of the three countries.
— has basic knowledge of the geography and climate of the Maghreb.

History
— knows when each of the three countries gained its independence from France (e.g., Morocco and Tunisia in 1956, Algeria in 1962).
— can identify the historical figures related to the independence of the Maghreb (e.g., Ben Bella, Bourguiba, al-Fasi, and Mohammed V).

Literature and the Arts
— can name some French writers and/or artists of Maghrebi origin (e.g., Mohammed Dib, Mouloud Feraoun, Katib Yacine).

Upon completing STAGE 3, the learner:

Communication in Cultural Context
— recognizes differences between continental French and the French spoken by North Africans and has little difficulty understanding these speakers.

The Value System
— understands that the interaction between male friends and relatives is particularly passionate in Maghrebi societies.
— is familiar with the Maghrebi concept of space in human relations, i.e., their preference for closer personal distances.

Social Patterns and Conventions
— is aware of the respect due the patriarch in the family.
— can describe the concept of extended family in Maghrebi societies.
— knows of the tendency to rely on close relatives for assistance (and is aware of the responsibilities of the patriarch with respect to his extended family).
— recognizes the significance of Maghrebi immigrants in France and can describe their socio-political and cultural impact on French society.

Social Institutions
— can assess the importance of tourism to the economies of Morocco and Tunisia and its impact on the local mores (e.g., consumption of alcohol in hotels and restaurants, effects on the younger generation of the European tourists' lack of modesty on the local beaches).
— can identify the form of government in each of the three countries (e.g., the Republic of Algeria, the Republic of Tunisia, and the Kingdom of Morocco).
— has basic knowledge of the main political parties in the three countries.
— can evaluate the political strength and social influence of the Islamist movements in the Maghreb.
— knows the status of polygamy in the three countries (e.g., forbidden in Tunisia, largely a rural phenomenon in Algeria and Morocco).

Geography and the Environment
— can locate, identify, and describe important regions of the Maghreb (e.g., the aridity of the Sahara desert in the South vs. the fertility of the Mediterranean coast line in the East and North, and the Atlantic ocean in the West; the Atlas mountains and its highest peak, Toubkal, in Morocco).
— can describe the most important natural resources of the Maghreb (e.g., oil and natural gas in Algeria, phosphate in Morocco and Tunisia).

— can explain the Maghreb's geopolitically strategic location (e.g., borders both the Mediterranean and the Atlantic, natural harbors situated only a few minutes from continental Europe).

History
— can demonstrate general knowledge of the history of France's colonial empire in the Maghreb (e.g., conquest of Algiers in 1830, the first settlers, and the ensuing war of "pacification"; extension of France's colonial rule over Tunisia in 1881 and Morocco in 1912).

— can distinguish between the "civilizing mission" and the French economic expansion as driving forces for the colonization of the Maghreb.

Literature and the Arts
— can identify and discuss works by major literary figures in the Maghreb who contributed to French literature (e.g., Katib Yacine, Ben Jelloun, Mohammed Dib, Mouloud Memmeri).

— has some knowledge of traditional architecture (e.g., houses with open sky court yards, tile walls and floors, absence of statues on buildings, decoration of houses and buildings with Arabic calligraphy).

Upon completing STAGE 4, the learner:

Communication in Cultural Context
— can distinguish between a lack of competency in the French language and a simple difference in accent in the spoken French of North Africans.

— is aware of the influence of Arabic on the French language and can give some examples of borrowed vocabulary (e.g., "toubib," "bled," "kif-kif,").

The Value System
— can explain the ambivalence of the younger Maghrebi generations toward France (admiration and resentment) in the light of France's technological prowess and economic prosperity on the one hand, and the colonial history of their countries on the other.

— can explain the feeling among Maghrebi people of both moral and cultural superiority vis-à-vis the West (e.g., Islam as the perfect religion for all humanity, Arabo-Islamic past achievements in the areas of the sciences, medicine, philosophy, and literature which preceded European enlightenment by half a millenium).

— can discuss local attitudes toward Western values in the light of economic disparities between North and South (e.g., resentment of stern neoimperialism and criticism of Western support of non-democratic regimes in North Africa).

Social Patterns and Conventions
— can assess the difference in acculturation between the well-educated segment of Maghrebi society and the less educated (e.g., adoption of Western attire and observance of non-Moslem festivals like the "réveillon" by the educated class).

— can discuss the status of women in each country (e.g., Tunisia's Personal Status Code of 1956, Islamist threat to the rights of women in Algeria, government support for women's associations in the three countries, participation of women in high-level government positions, election to the legislature in Morocco).

— is familiar with women's organizations and leading women intellectuals in the Maghreb (e.g., Union de la Femme Tunisienne).
— can discuss local gender relations without resorting to stereotypes (e.g., North African women are beginning to become an important social and economic force, and their exclusion has more to do with male-dominated international and local systems than with an inherent deficiency in the North African culture).

Social Institutions
— can discuss the principal economic activities of each country and evaluate their economic well-being (e.g., oil and natural gas exports and agriculture in Algeria; textile, small industries, tourism, and agriculture in Tunisia and Morocco).
— can evaluate in some depth current manifestations of the impact of French culture on the local societies.
— can discuss the current evolution of political and social institutions (e.g., legal opposition movements, labor unions, legislative elections, role of the military).
— can discuss the role of bilingual education in Tunisia and Morocco (e.g., all science subjects are taught in French at the high school and university levels; official documents are in both French and Arabic).
— can discuss Algeria's "Arabization" program.

Geography and the Environment
— can discuss the question of water in the three countries.
— can identify the location of major centers of natural resources (e.g., oil fields of Hasi Masoud in Algeria, phosphate mines in Rdeif in Tunisia).

History
— can discuss at length the struggle for independence and identify the role played by the main nationalist leaders in each country as well as their respective political organizations (e.g., Bourguiba's Neodestour party, Algeria's FLN, and al-Fasi's Independence party).
— can analyze the significance of the Algerian Revolution and relate the "Algerian Question" to events such as the fall of the Fourth Republic, General de Gaulle's return to power, and the advent of the Fifth Republic.
— can situate the independence movements in the international context (e.g., international recognition of Algeria's revolution and its negative effect on France's prestige).
— can demonstrate how the religious and socio-political history of the Maghreb has contributed to the creation of conflicting cultural traits and values (see "The Value System" above).

Literature and the Arts
— is familiar with typical art forms and artistic production in the Maghreb (e.g., Carthage international film festival, North African films like *Halfaouine* by the Tunisian Farid Boughdir, and productions by the Algerian Lakhdhar Hamina).
— can differentiate between Islamic and European influence in architecture and arts (e.g., modest inward North African buildings and houses versus high and outward European structures and villas).

— can demonstrate knowledge of major themes of Francophone Maghrebi literature and of the works where they are found.
— is aware that the upper Maghrebi social classes are drawn to French (European) high culture, while the popular classes, constituting a large majority, are primarily interested in the art, music, and literature of the Middle East, centered in Egypt.

PART III

CULTURAL COMPETENCE: GRADES 9-12

*Coordinators: Ali Moeller, University of Nebraska-Lincoln
Renée White, Greenhill School, Dallas, Texas*

The purpose of this section is to adapt the guidelines for competence in French culture, presented in the preceding chapters, to learners at the high school level. Since students come from varied language experiences (FLES, FLEX, immersion, partial immersion), the level of competence the students will achieve in a given grade, from 9 to 12, depends on their previous background in the target culture.

Generally, high school students enrolled in foreign language courses attend class daily for approximately forty-five minutes. Under normal circumstances, they may be expected to complete, in four years, Stage 2 of cultural competence as defined in the set of cultural indicators given below. Students who start study of the target culture before high school, however, or are in an AP or IB program, may reach Stage 3 in some areas of competence.

Knowledge about French culture, when not based on direct contact with a Francophone country, should be rooted whenever possible in exposure to authentic materials such as literature, introduce films and video documents, and a wide range of artifacts. Teachers should take advantage of current events to extend beyond Europe and present cultural aspects of other French-speaking communities around the world (e.g., in North America, Europe, Africa, the Caribbean, etc.).

High school students differ from elementary and middle school students in their greater ability to reflect about the things they observe and experience. In the study of culture at this level, consequently, considerable emphasis should be accorded critical thinking, rather than just the acquisition of a body of knowledge—although knowledge is certainly essential. The pedagogical approach should thus be chosen with a view toward sharpening the students' ability to observe and analyze cultural phenomena, while cultivating the capacity for empathy toward the target culture. Teachers should consult carefully the goals in these areas given in Part II of this report, Understanding Culture.

To achieve these objectives, it helps to encourage reflection, as well, on the students' own culture in comparison to the target culture, focussing on both similarities and differences. Observation and analysis of one's own culture, in which both the common purposes between people and their diversity is recognized, helps to eliminate the either this way or that way mentality. The result is a more open and nonjudgmental approach to observing a second culture. The awareness and acceptance of cultural diversity becomes a life-long perspective, not a mere gathering of facts about individual cultures.

INDICATORS OF COMPETENCE

Upon completing STAGE 1 (FRENCH I AND II), the learner:

Communication in Cultural Context
— knows what verbal behavior is appropriate in different greeting and leave-taking routines (e.g., "Bonjour, Madame" vs. "Salut, Jean").
— knows appropriate titles of address (e.g., "Monsieur, Madame, Mademoiselle, Monsieur l'agent, docteur").
— knows formulas of politeness (e.g., "Merci, S'il vous plaît, Je vous en prie").
— knows some appropriate expressions of well-wishing (e.g., "A tes/vos souhaits" when someone sneezes).
— knows the appropriate way of writing the date in French.
— knows that there are familiar and polite forms of address ("tu" vs. "vous").
— can convey an attitude of goodwill via tone of voice.
— recognizes some easily interpreted gestures (e.g., hand-waving in greetings or leave-taking, cupping the ear, thumbs up or down).

Social Patterns and Conventions
— knows some typical French names.
— can identify the day of the week using a French calendar (knows that the French week begins on Monday).
— is aware of the difference between the "first floor" in U.S. homes or buildings and the "premier étage" in France.
— can describe the basic conventions governing greeting and leave-taking as regards the age and sex of those being greeted and social relationships (e.g., a handshake vs. kissing on the cheek when greeting).
— knows that table manners are different in France (e.g., knows how the French place their hands when eating).
— can describe daily French meal patterns (lunch and dinner).
— can describe the order of dishes in a traditional French meal.
— can identify some major foods and culinary products (e.g., baguettes, croissants, crême caramel).
— can say which kinds of traditional French neighborhood stores sell what kind of merchandise.

— can identify traditional French sports (e.g., soccer, cycling, "la pétanque").
— can identify sports in other Francophone areas (e.g., hockey in Quebec, "la pelote" in the Basque country).
— knows the difference between one's "fête" and one's birthday.
— knows how to count on the fingers in the French manner (beginning with the thumb).
— is aware that certain numbers are written differently in France (e.g., 1, 4, and 7).

Social Institutions
— can identify the French flag.
— recognizes the French national anthem and knows that it is called "La Marseillaise."
— is aware of some French holidays and how they are celebrated (e.g., July 14, Christmas, Mardi Gras, Easter).
— can use French currency, or replicas thereof, to "purchase" goods and make change.
— can calculate the value of U.S. currency in French francs.
— can name major modes of public transportation (e.g., métro, taxi, bus, train, avion).
— can understand time using the 24-hour clock.
— can understand temperature readings (cold, warm, hot) using the Celsius thermometer.
— can name the major school levels (from the "maternelle" to the "lycée") and knows the corresponding ages of the students.

Geography and the Environment
— can find France on a map of Europe.
— knows that there are French departments outside metropolitan France (in the Caribbean and elsewhere) and can name a few.
— knows that there are French-speaking culture areas in Switzerland and Belgium and can find those countries and the relevant areas on a map of Europe.
— can identify on a map of Europe all the countries bordering France.
— knows that French is spoken in Canada (Quebec) and can locate Quebec on a map of North America.
— knows that French is an official language in certain countries in North and Sub-Saharan Africa and can identify one or two of those countries.
— knows that French is an official language in Haiti.

History
— knows that a great number of English words have a French origin (e.g., "denim" from "toile de Nîmes," "chowder" from "chaudière," "curfew" from "couvre-feu").
— can name and identify a few major historical landmarks and monuments of Paris (e.g., Notre Dame de Paris, Arc de Triomphe, Tour Eiffel).
— can name and identify a few major landmarks outside of Paris (e.g., le Mont-Saint-Michel, Versailles).
— can name a few famous French historical figures who made significant contributions to the U.S. (e.g., Marquette, Lafayette, Rochambeau).

Literature and Arts
— can identify a few famous authors and artists (e.g., Hugo, Rodin, Manet).
— can recognize a few common folk songs.

Upon completing STAGE 2 (FRENCH III AND IV), the learner:

Communication in Cultural Context
— can distinguish between linguistic registers appropriate to formal and informal social settings (e.g., having a coke at a cafe with a friend and dining with a friend's family).
— demonstrates knowledge of some expressions used in informal settings (e.g., when talking with friends: "C'est génial!"; "J'ai bien bossé hier soir").
— demonstrates knowledge of some common formulas used in telephone conversations (e.g., "Allô," "C'est moi," "Ne quittez pas," "Je vous la passe").
— knows a few formulas necessary for writing letters in French.
— is aware of the difference in personal space needed by French and Americans in face-to-face conversations (the French feel comfortable at a somewhat closer distance than is customary for Americans).
— can interpret some common French gestures.
— is familiar with a few French proverbs as compared with their English equivalents (e.g., "Un tiens vaut mieux que deux tu l'auras" = "A bird in the hand is worth two in the bush").
— is aware that French is perceived in both Africa and the Caribbean as the language of the elite and of social advancement.
— is aware that there are differences in vocabulary and pronunciation between standard French and the French spoken in other Francophone countries, and understands that these differences reflect cultural variations and merit respect.
— is aware that French is, with English, the official language used at the Olympic Games.
— is aware that French is one of the official languages used at the United Nations.

The Value System
— can identify at least three central values and some related thought patterns or assumptions (e.g., the value of "friendship" and the tendency toward distrust of outsiders exhibited in the French hesitancy to invite new acquaintances into their home; the value of "the art of living" as reflected in the cult of gastronomy, the art of conversation, and generous annual paid vacations; the value of individualism and freedom as reflected in the practice of the "système D").

Social Patterns and Conventions
— knows the importance of hand shaking in greeting and leave-taking.
— can describe briefly several French social conventions (e.g., table manners, gift giving when invited to a French home).
— can describe several social conventions of the youth culture (e.g. going out with a group of friends rather than "dating", meeting at cafés, going to "boums" and "soirées").
— is aware that French secondary school students, unlike their American counterparts, do not have part-time jobs.

— is aware that French teenagers do not have their own cars.
— is aware of the importance of the evening meal as a family tradition, although the larger meal is often taken at noon.
— knows that menus are displayed outside French restaurants.
— knows how to order a meal from a French menu.
— is aware that many French people now do grocery shopping in a large *hypermarché* (combination supermarket and department store) rather than in the traditional neighborhood stores.
— understands the difference between "les toilettes" (les WC) and "la salle de bain(s)".
— can identify some foods from Francophone countries other than France (e.g., *couscous* and *méchoui* from North Africa).

Social Institutions
— can describe how some additional major holidays are celebrated (e.g., New Year's Eve, "la fête des Rois," Labor Day).
— can explain how to use public transportation in France (e.g., using the métro in Paris, taking a train).
— is familiar with the basic measurements used in France (e.g., meter, kilogram, litre).
— knows how periods and commas are used in French numbers (e.g., "1,5 kgs"; "2.500 or 2 500 francs").
— knows the secondary school grade level designations (from "6ème" to "Terminale").
— can describe the grading system in French schools (e.g., grading on 10 or 20 pts.).
— knows how the organization of the school week in France is different in public as opposed to parochial schools.
— is aware of some differences between the French and American school systems (e.g., the role and importance of the French baccalaureat exam, municipally organized vs. school sports).
— can name the current president and at least one other important political figure of France.

Geography and the Environment
— can identify the major cities of France on an outline map.
— can place on a map of France the principal mountain ranges, rivers, and surrounding bodies of water.
— can name a few countries in North and Sub-Saharan Africa in which French is spoken.
— can name French departments and French-speaking countries in the Caribbean.

History
— can name an event in each of the major periods—Middle Ages, 16th Century, etc.—of the history of France (Guerre de Cent Ans, Edit de Nantes, Revolution, Occupation).
— can identify at least one prominent historical personality linked to each of the above events (Jeanne d'Arc, Henri IV, Louis XVI, de Gaulle).
— knows that Morocco, Algeria, and Tunisia are, with some African and Caribbean countries, former French colonies or protectorates.

Scientific and Technological Achievements
— knows what the "TGV" is and is aware of the magnitude of the Franco-British feat in constructing the Channel tunnel (le "Chunnel").
— can name at least three famous French scientists and their contributions (e.g., Pasteur—pasteurization and anti-rabies inoculation; Marie Curie—radium; Professor Luc Montagnier—AIDS research).
— is aware that France holds fourth place in the world for the number of Nobel prizes received (literature, peace, sciences, and medicine).

Literature and the Arts
— can identify three major authors (e.g., Voltaire, Molière, Camus) and one work by each of them (e.g., *Candide, Le Bourgeois Gentilhomme, l'Etranger*).
— can identify a few additional major artists and/or musicians (e.g., Debussy, Renoir, Monet).
— knows the name of one or two contemporary singers or bands in France.
— can identify a well-known Francophone cartoon series (e.g., Astérix, Tintin).

Upon completing STAGE 3 (PRIMARILY FRENCH 5, AP, AND 1B PROGRAMS), the learner:

Communication in Cultural Context
— can express gratitude appropriately (e.g., "Je vous remercie, Madame").
— knows how to apologize appropriately according to the situation (e.g., bumping into someone: "Oh, excusez-moi!"; arriving late: "Je suis désolé").
— knows how to accept compliments appropriately (e.g., "Vous trouvez?" instead of the American "Thank you.")
— recognizes current physical gestures that accompany or evoke some common colloquialisms (e.g., "Mon oeil", "Il est cinglé!").

Social Patterns and Conventions
— is aware of the similarities and differences between French and American child-rearing practices (e.g., attitude toward upbringing, kinds of discipline, activities with their parents, attitude toward school work).
— is aware of the distinction between practicing and nonpracticing Catholics in France.

Social Institutions
— knows that there are many different baccalaureats, as opposed to the uniform American high school diploma, and can identify some of the main categories (e.g., Bac L, OR "Lettres," and Bac S, OR "Scientifique").
— is aware that French banknotes feature likenesses of literary and artistic figures (e.g., St.-Exupéry on the 50F bill) in contrast to the pictures of Presidents on American money.
— can describe the main religious groups in France (e.g., Catholics, Protestants, Jews, and Moslems).
— is aware that the Napoleonic Code is still used in Louisiana.

Geography
— can identify on a map some major cities of Francophone countries/areas outside Europe.

Literature and the Arts
— can identify at least two major authors from Francophone countries and at least one work from each of them (e.g. Gabrielle Roy, *Rue Deschambault,* Aimé Césaire, "Soleil Cou Coupé").
— knows the names of some French authors in addition to those learned in Stages 1 and 2, as well as the title of at least one of their works.

Scientific and Technological Achievements
— can name some additional important recent achievements of the French scientific community (e.g., the Concorde supersonic jet, the Ariane rocket).
— can name some additional contributions by French scientists or inventors (e.g., Daguerre and photography, the Lumière brothers and motion pictures, Lavoisier and chemistry).

PART IV

CULTURAL COMPETENCE: KINDERGARTEN THROUGH EIGHTH GRADE

Coordinator: Katherine Kurk, Northern Kentucky University

In this section we propose a sequence of cultural objectives correlated with the cognitive development of students from kindergarten through eighth grade. In recognition of the importance of interdisciplinary foreign language and culture instruction, curriculum objectives of the general course of study in elementary and middle schools are integrated into the following set of indicators wherever appropriate. Coordination with social studies is particularly rewarding, since major themes are frequently adopted locally for each grade level.

The indicators of competence have been organized into two broad levels: kindergarten to grade 4 and grades 5 to 8. This grouping was chosen in anticipation of national testing of basic school subjects at grades 4 and 8 in accordance with the proposed National Standards in Foreign Language Education guidelines. From kindergarten to grade 5 it is assumed that classes in French meet at least three times a week for a minimum of 75 minutes per week, while in middle school they meet daily for 45-minute periods. The grades 5–8 core of indicators accomodates this change of pace at grade 6 by leaving complete latitude to the teachers regarding the number and order of tasks they will have their students undertake. We recognize that K–8 programs are often geared to overall curriculum designs and that instructors may need to organize their French instruction accordingly. We also realize that some FLES* Program models, such as FLEX, which have fewer contact hours, cannot meet all of the goals suggested below.

Moreover, the variety of FLES* programs requires a distinction between the basic core and what may be called an accelerated core. The latter refers mainly to immersion programs, of which there are few thus far in the United States, but may include any program which reaches beyond the basic core. More ambitious K–8 programs can challenge some of the tasks that belong to Stage 2, as is illustrated in the additional objectives for accelerated programs presented after the basic core. It is considered, however, that meeting the Stage 1 objectives in K–8 is an adequate foundation for a coherent learning sequence continuing into high school and college.

Teachers in programs which begin later than K–4 will want to incorporate all of the basic core indicators proposed for that level, adapting the presentation to the learners' age level. This is facilitated by the "spiraling" built into the succession of indicators. At the beginning, for instance, students are asked to be able to identify French money, then to be able to make "purchases" with French money or replicas, and finally, in higher grades they are expected to be able to calculate the value of dollars in French francs.

While this sequence of indicators was written with the expectation that culture instruction will take place in French, individual program goals and teacher judgment will determine whether French or English will be used and at which level.

And finally, while France is central to the target language and culture, teachers are regularly encouraged by the indicators to take their students beyond the typical Eurocentric perspective to a knowledge and appreciation of some of the other important Francophone cultures around the globe. It is recommended that teachers take every opportunity offered by the social studies connection, by current events, or by the ethnic composition of the class, to extend the horizon beyond Europe and the U.S.

Note: This section is deeply indebted to contributions by Dr. Myriam Met and her research associate, Eileen Lorenz (Montgomery County Public Schools, Rockville, MD).

INDICATORS OF COMPETENCE FOR GRADES K–4

Upon completing Grade 4, the learner:

Communication in Cultural Context
— recognizes some easily interpreted gestures (e.g., hand-waving in greetings or leave-taking, cupping the ear, thumbs up or down).
— demonstrates understanding of selected terms of endearment used among family members in France (e.g., "mon chéri," "mon chou," "ma puce").
— knows what verbal behavior is appropriate in different greeting and leave-taking routines (e.g., "Bonjour, Madame" vs. "Salut, Jean").
— can respond verbally to requests, using appropriate language according to age and relationship of the interlocutor (e.g., "Oui, Madame" vs. "O.K"!).
— knows there are familiar and polite/plural forms of address ("tu"/"vous").

Social Patterns and Conventions
— can use appropriate gestures upon greeting and leave-taking (shaking hands or kissing on the cheek).
— can identify the day of the week using a French calendar (knows that the French week begins on Monday).
— can identify some typical foods of France and other French-speaking areas, including those related to holidays (e.g., crêpes, baguettes, cheeses, couscous, maple syrup in Quebec).
— uses age-appropriate table manners.
— can describe daily French meal patterns.

— knows how to sing the French equivalent of "Happy Birthday".
— is aware of some French holidays and how they are celebrated (e.g., July 14, Christmas, Mardi Gras, Pâques).
— knows some typical French names.
— can identify some sports popular in French-speaking countries (e.g., soccer, cycling, rugby, "la pétanque," skiing).
— can recognize the French numeral abbreviation of the date (e.g., 21/3/95).
— knows how to count on the fingers in the French manner (beginning with the thumb).
— is aware that certain numbers are written differently in France (e.g., 1 and 7).

Social Institutions
— can identify the flag of France and/or of a Francophone country.
— recognizes the French national anthem and knows that it is called "La Marseillaise."
— can identify currency and coins from France and/or a Francophone country.
— can identify major modes of public transportation (e.g., "métro," taxi, bus, train and "TGV").
— knows that French children go to school just as American children do and learn many of the same subjects.
— shows awareness of differences between the American and French school week and vacations.
— knows that both the nuclear and extended families are important in France as in the U.S. and knows appropriate vocabulary (e.g., "mère," "grand-mère," "oncle," etc.).
— can identify a major symbol of France (e.g., Eiffel Tower, fleur-de-lis, the Gallic rooster).

Geography and the Environment
— can locate France on a world map in relation to the U.S.
— can identify the capital of France and locate it on a map.
— can state the relative size of France (roughly as large as Texas).
— can describe the general climate in selected regions of France (e.g., relatively warm in the Midi, cooler in the North, a lot of snow in the Alps and Pyrenees) with the aid of a map.
— can locate one additional Francophone country on a world map and is aware that French is the principal language there.
— can identify, where relevant, a French sister-city to the students' own town.
— is aware of French-speaking communities (if any) in the student's own city or state.
— can name some U.S. cities with French names (e.g., St. Louis, New Orleans, Des Moines, Terre Haute, etc.).
— is aware of the ethnic and religious diversity of France and of the Francophone world.

History
— can identify some major historical landmarks and monuments of France (e.g., Mont-Saint-Michel, l'Arc de Triomphe).
— can name and briefly describe the contributions of selected important historical figures (e.g., Jeanne d'Arc, Napoleon).
— can name selected French or Francophone explorers, soldiers, or politicians with connections to the United States (e.g., Marquette, Joliet, La Salle, La Fayette).

Literature and the Arts
— can recite and use gestures to express understanding of traditional French songs (e.g., "Meunier, tu dors!," "Savez-vous planter les choux?").
— can recite some French nursery rhymes ("comptines"), with the typical "jump rope" rhythm (e.g., "Un, deux, trois, je vais dans les bois," "Une souris verte," "Une poule sur un mur").
— can perform simple folk dances from Francophone countries (e.g., "Sur le pont d'Avignon").
— is familiar with stories about famous characters in French children's literature (e.g., Babar, Tintin, les Schtroumpfs).
— can relate a tale, legend, or fable known to children of a French-speaking country (e.g., La Fontaine's fables).
— can identify the arts and crafts of several French-speaking countries (e.g., French santons, African weavings, basketry).

INDICATORS OF COMPETENCE FOR GRADES K-8

Upon completing Grade 8, the learner:

Communication in Cultural Context
— can use familiar and polite/plural forms of address ("tu" vs. "vous") appropriately.
— is aware of difference in demeanor in formal and informal social settings (e.g., having refreshments in a café among friends vs. dining with a French friend's family).
— shows awareness that there are linguistic differences (vocabulary, pronunciation) between "standard" French and the French spoken in some regions of France (e.g., the Midi) and in other Francophone countries, and understands that these differences reflect cultural variations which all merit respect.

Social Patterns and Conventions
— can identify traditional French costumes and knows that this clothing is worn only for holidays and festivals.
— is aware of the difference between the "first floor" in U.S. homes or buildings and the "premier étage" in France.
— understands the difference between "les toilettes" ("les WC") and "la salle de bain(s)" as regards sanitary facilities in France.
— can identify eating experiences as opportunities for social interaction.
— can describe the weekly market and explain its role in French life.
— can identify selected French stores (e.g., "la boulangerie," "la boucherie," "le tabac," "le supermarché," "le grand magasin").
— can identify kinds of merchandise with the stores in which they are sold (e.g., bread and the "boulangerie," stamps and the post office or the "bureau de tabac").
— shows awareness of daily French meal patterns (scheduling of lunch and dinner).
— can describe the order of dishes served in a traditional French meal (e.g., "entrée, plat principal, salade verte, fromage, dessert").

— knows the difference between one's "fête" and one's birthday.
— can identify leisure activities (in addition to sports) popular with peers in France.
— can name some popular figures of French sports or entertainment.

Social Institutions
— knows how additional holidays are celebrated in France (or another Francophone country) and in the U.S. (e.g., New Year's Eve, Labor Day, Armistice Day).
— can use French currency, or replicas thereof, to "purchase" goods and make change.
— can calculate the value of U.S. currency in French francs.
— can understand time using the 24-hour clock.
— knows that the metric system is used in France (as well as in the rest of Europe) and is familiar with some of the principal measures (e.g., knows that a kilometer is a thousand meters and can compare kilometers with miles and meters with yards; knows that a kilogram is a thousand grams and can compare kilograms and pounds).
— can understand temperature readings (cold, warm, hot) using the Celsius thermometer.
— can name the major types of schools (from the "maternelle" to the "lycée") and knows the ages of the students at each level.
— knows the grade level designations, starting with the "6ème".
— can describe the grading system in French schools (e.g., grading on 10 or 20 points).
— is familiar with a typical week's schedule for a French student her/his age.
— can name community helpers in Francophone countries (e.g., agents de police, facteurs, pompiers).
— can purchase a ticket for the metro, train, and bus.
— can understand simple public signs and instructions.

Geography and the Environment
— can place two or three of the principal mountain ranges and rivers of France on an outline map and identify the bodies of water which surround it.
— can identify on a map the countries bordering France, using their French names, and can say which have French-speaking communities.
— can locate some French-speaking countries outside of Europe and North America (e.g., in North Africa and Sub-Saharan West Africa).
— can locate the French-speaking areas in the Caribbean (e.g., Martinique, Guadeloupe, Haiti, La Guyane).
— can identify and locate some of the major cities in France besides the capital.
— can identify and name flora and fauna in France and other Francophone countries.
— shows awareness of environmental concerns of one French-speaking country.

History
— can name and identify five major historical events and related landmarks or monuments of France.
— can identify events that led to initial contacts between France and the New World, and can name some of the early settlements in the U.S. and Canada.

- can identify patterns of settlement of immigrants from French-speaking areas to the U.S. (e.g., French Canadians to New England and Louisiana).
- can identify the contributions of some French or Francophone men and/or women (e.g., Louis Pasteur, Marie Curie, Leopold Senghor).
- knows that the French-speaking countries of North Africa (the Maghreb) and Sub-Saharan West Africa were formerly part of the French empire.
- knows that Martinique, Guadeloupe, and La Guyane, former French colonies, are now departments of France (much as Alaska and Hawaii are States).
- can indicate how modern technology has changed the way people live in France and/or another Francophone country.

Literature and the Arts
- can identify some important Francophone authors and artists.
- can identify selected works of French art.
- knows some contemporary songs from France and/or Francophone countries.

GRADES K THROUGH 8: OPTIONAL SUPPLEMENTARY OBJECTIVES

INDICATORS OF COMPETENCE FOR GRADES K-4 (ACCELERATED PROGRAMS)

Upon completing Grade 4, the learner:

Communication in Cultural Context
- understands the difference between familiar ("tu") and polite ("vous") forms of address in French and usually uses them appropriately.
- can use appropriate gestures upon greeting and leave-taking (e.g., shaking hands or kissing on the cheek).
- can create a "carte de voeux" for New Year's or a thank you letter using appropriate formulas.

Social Patterns and Conventions
- can describe the order of dishes served in a traditional French meal.
- can identify, name and describe items of French cuisine and knows when they are appropriately used or served.
- can name and describe places where people can purchase foods in France.
- can identify and name places (e.g., "boutiques," "supermarchés") in France where clothing may be purchased.
- can name and describe leisure activities popular with peers in France and Francophone countries.

— can name and describe traditional French sports and some popular figures of French sports.

Social Institutions
— can identify flags and/or symbols of several Francophone countries.

Geography and the Environment
— can locate some Francophone countries on a globe or map.
— is aware of French-speaking communities (if any) in the student's own city or state.
— can place the principal mountain ranges and rivers of France on an outline map and identify the bodies of water which surround it.

History
— can name, identify, and describe five or more major historical landmarks and monuments of France.
— can name selected important French or Francophone historical figures and discuss their importance.

Literature and the Arts
— can identify and appreciate illustrations in French children's literature as an expression of French culture and could use such illustrations to tell a story.
— knows a few simple contemporary songs from France or from Francophone countries.

INDICATORS OF COMPETENCE FOR GRADES 5-8 (ACCELERATED PROGRAMS)

Upon completing Grade 8, the learner:

Communication in Cultural Context
— uses appropriate titles of address and formula in survival-level situations (e.g., "S'il vous plaît" to accompany a request or call a waiter, "Merci" to acknowledge a service).
— demonstrates knowledge of common formulas used in answering the telephone (e.g., "C'est moi-même," "Ne quittez pas, je vous la passe," "Je regrette, il/elle n'est pas là").
— understands that there is a difference between the use of written and spoken language in France (e.g., the use of "ça" vs. "cela").
— accepts compliments appropriately (e.g., "Vous trouvez?" instead of the American "Thank you").

Social Patterns and Conventions
— is aware of gift-giving customs when invited to a French home (e.g., offering candy or flowers—but not chrysanthemums).
— knows how to use table manners and to identify table settings appropriate to French culture.
— understands relationships between parent-child and adult-child in France.

— can identify and explain how modern technology has changed the way people live in France (e.g., Minitel, the "TGV").

Social Institutions
— understands temperatures measured in both Fahrenheit and centigrade and how to calculate equivalencies.
— knows how periods and commas are used in French numbers (e.g., 1,5 kgs; 2.500 or 2 500 francs).
— can describe the structure of the extended family in France.
— understands how public communication systems link citizens nationally and internationally.
— is aware of some differences between French and American schools (e.g., student-teacher relationships, limited role of sports in French schools).
— can name the current President and Prime Minister of France and of one other Francophone country.
— can compare the legislative branches of government in France and U.S. (e.g., "Assemblée nationale" and "Sénat"; House of Representatives and Senate) and knows that a member of the "Assemblée nationale" is called a "député").
— can name the dominant religions practiced in France.
— knows that certain festivals and holidays have a religious origin and can describe some of them as practiced.
— can name some major industries of France (e.g., wines, cheeses, perfume, fashion, automobiles, aeronautics, petrochemicals, communications).
— understands the importance of economics in the interdependence of the U.S., France, and other Francophone countries.

Geography and the Environment
— can name some of the better-known regions of France (e.g., Normandy, Brittany, Burgundy, Provence, etc.).
— can identify and locate the capitals of several other French-speaking countries in and outside of Europe (e.g., Brussels, Geneva, Algiers, Abidjan), and describe them.
— can describe, generally, the topographical characteristics of some French-speaking countries outside of France (e.g., the Alps in Switzerland, the desert in North Africa, the savanna and jungle in Sub-Saharan West Africa).
— can name important natural resources of France.
— can name some regions in France identified with particular products (e.g., camembert from Normandy, lace-making in Brittany, red wine from Burgundy, "santons" from Provence).
— can explain how the natural environment has influenced the way French people meet their needs (vegetation, animal life, water resources, soil).
— can identify environmental concerns in France or another Francophone country.

History
— can give some information about several of the generally accepted periods in the history of France (e.g., Hundred Years' War, Renaissance, Revolution, Occupation).

— can name some prominent historical personalities linked to the above (e.g., Jeanne d'Arc, François Ier, Louis XVI, Pétain, De Gaulle).

— can compare the roles of various modes of transportation in France and the U.S. from early settlement to modern times.

Literature and the Arts

— can identify selected styles of French architecture (e.g., Roman and Gothic cathedrals).

— can identify and describe works by some Francophone authors (e.g., *La Belle et la Bête, Le Petit Prince, Le Petit Nicolas, Astérix*).

— can name and discuss an age-appropriate French or Francophone film (e.g., *Le Ballon rouge, Les Douze Travaux d'Astérix*).

PART V

TESTING CULTURAL COMPETENCE

Coordinators: Walter H. Bartz, Indiana Department of Education
Rosalie A. Vermette, Indiana University-Purdue University, Indianapolis

In the field of foreign language education, culture has always been considered an important and an inseparable component of language learning. Finding ways to assess student progress in the learning of culture, however, has been very difficult and time-consuming for the teacher in the classroom and for those who develop external, standardized assessment tools.

The development of assessment tools or testing instruments cannot be done in isolation. Assessment, curriculum, and instruction are highly interrelated, to the extent that a change or adjustment in any one will and should affect the others. The development of instruments to assess cultural learning will necessarily need to take into account the desired learning outcomes, or curricular goals, and the instruction that is carried out in language classrooms—which, in the view of most educators, are the appropriate bases for assessment. Assessment, however, should not determine what the curricular goals and/or instruction are to be. Once it is determined what is it that students should know and be able to do, appropriate instructional strategies are carried out and assessment tools are designed to evaluate the progress of the students in meeting the expected outcomes.

The assessment prototypes described in this section are governed by the following principles:

Principle 1. While a language and its culture interact, the assessment of cultural proficiency should focus as narrowly and as clearly as possible on measuring the cultural component of an interaction. Thus, for example, tests measuring sociolinguistic ability must assess the acceptability of behaviors independently **but** within a language context. For example, within the task of "greetings," the cultural measure should look at kinetic factors such as appropriateness of gestures and distance, as well as linguistic register, but without focusing on linguistic correctness per se.

Principle 2. Assessment of cultural knowledge (cognitive skills) should include aspects of life style (small "c") and civilization (large "C"), but these should be evaluated as distinct features. While traditional achievement-type items are acceptable, consideration should be given to learners' exhibiting their abilities to integrate this knowledge into wider contexts. Dossier or portfolio presentations might provide evidence of learners' perspectives on a time or place within the culture.

Principle 3. Assessment of cultural awareness and behaviors should be innovative and predicated on creative designs. It should be task-oriented, with preference given to direct measures where possible. Examples: reports of learners' observations when viewing or reading about the target culture; reports about learners' behaviors in simulations and real life interaction.

Principle 4. Any test battery must clearly state the purpose of the measurement and the contribution made by this aspect to the learners' total cultural competence. Assessment tasks must be designed to be appropriate for the age of the learner, thereby necessitating developmentally appropriate strategies for elementary school, middle school, high school, and adult learners.

"Multiple-choice" tests are an obvious, easily-scored method for testing learned information. However, to assess higher-level thinking such as interpretation and analysis, "multiple-choice" tests are limited in their ability to serve as direct measures of cultural behaviors. Therefore, the prototypes described below present a variety of assessment methods. Many of these prototypes can be used to assess cultural competence in more than the area under which they are listed. By changing the focus of the information given in the item, different kinds of knowledge can be evaluated about different kinds of Francophone cultures. The questions given under various prototypes are only examples and are in no way exhaustive.

A. GENERAL

Type 1. Portfolio Assessment

Portfolio assessment is a unique test prototype and is perhaps the most comprehensive method of observing and documenting a student's progress over a period of time in many (but not all) areas of cultural competence.

Purpose: To assess the development of students' cultural proficiency over a period of time.

Method: A student portfolio is a collection of a student's work to show progress in developing cultural competence over a period of time such as a term, a year, or even over the complete school career.

Example: A student portfolio may contain a variety of evaluative documents such as personal essays, journal entries, or personal reflections based on a stay in the foreign culture; audio or video tapes showing the student's ability to perform appropriately within a cultural context; results of the student's research on cultural topics (both big "C" and little "c"); etc.

B. EMPATHY TOWARD OTHER CULTURES

Type 2. Semantic-differential test

Purpose: To test students' attitudes towards other cultures. A "semantic-differential" type of assessment can be devised in English and given to students beginning the study of another language. The same test can be administered at the end of the course (or the school year), or at the beginning of the next course (or school year) in which the student is enrolled. In this way changes in attitude can be observed in students.

Method: Arrange pairs of opposing adjectives in two columns; those characterizing a people favorably in one column and those characterizing them disparagingly in another (e.g., lazy / workaholic, beautiful / unattractive, outgoing / shy, etc.). Have students put their choice of **A**(-merican) or **F**(-rench), **A** or **FC**(French-Canadian), or **A** or **NA**(North African), etc. next to each antonym in the pairs of adjectives.

Reflections on intercultural attitudes can be stimulated by discussing the results of such tests.

Type 3. Cross-cultural "conflict situation"

Purpose: To see whether students can explain situational conflicts in which misunderstandings arise because of cross-cultural differences.

Method: Present a dialogue in which accusations are exchanged between two or more people from different cultural backgrounds and have students react to the culture-based conflict situation.

Example: An American goes to a French post office and wants to mail a package. After waiting in line for 15 minutes, she arrives at the window and is told that she must go to the window where packages are sent; this line is for letters only. The American refuses to go and screams that the French are stupid and have no idea what customer service means.

Questions: What defense against a given unfair accusation might win attention? What historical consideration or shared value might reveal common ground? How else could the hostility be defused?

C. KNOWLEDGE OF FRENCH-SPEAKING SOCIETIES

Type 4. Written or oral questions on appropriate behavior

Purpose: To assess students' comprehension of and adaptability to culturally distinct patterns of behavior in the other culture.

Method: Have students write brief answers to one or more questions on social conventions that govern conversation, dating, invitations to social events, and common formulas for social correspondence.

Example: John is visiting France for the first time on a student exchange program. Chantal, a French classmate, has invited him to an informal party attended by other French students whom he has met on a casual basis. When he arrives at the party, Chantal kisses him on both cheeks. John is surprised and somewhat embarrassed because he has only considered Chantal as a casual acquaintance. (He also has an American girlfriend back home who might be jealous!) Chantal senses his surprise and embarrassment and she is confused. In classroom interactions, John always sounds like such a friendly and sociable person—why is he acting so reticent now?

Questions: Explain why the misunderstanding arose between John and Chantal. Focus on the difference between John's and Chantal's assumptions about behavior (in an informal, social setting). Explain how John might have acted if he had had a better understanding of French behavior.

Type 5. Visual examples of authentic cultural situations

Purpose: To assess whether students can recognize and discuss a culture-based situation or behavior in print media, in art, in films, or in photos.

Method: Show a photo, drawing, painting, newspaper clipping, or film segment in which a culture pattern is illustrated.

Example: A picture showing a neighborhood café in Paris. Behind the counter can be seen bottles of alcoholic beverages. There are no barstools at the counter. The tables are tiny, round café tables typical of such places. At the counter, standing up, are a few people; some are drinking coffee from tiny demitasse (espresso) cups, while others are drinking apéritifs from ordinary drinking glasses. At a table in the background, a couple is eating a light meal (e.g., an omelette, or a sandwich on a demi-baguette, or a small steak with long, thin french fries). At another table in the background, a group of three or four is crowded around the tiny table, sharing a bottle of wine; the wine and half-full glasses can be seen. The people are sitting back comfortably in their chairs, engaged in converstion; two are smoking. In the foreground, two men are drinking espresso from two demitasse cups.

Questions: a) What does this exemplify? b) What cultural attitude can you identify here? c) Describe *two* aspects of the scene above which are NOT likely to apply to comparable American eating or drinking establishments. In your description, contrast the two types of places (American versus French) by focusing on features depicted above, such as the type of food or drink being consumed or the social function of the meeting place.

Type 6. Verbal description of a typical or an unlikely situation

Purpose: To assess whether students can recognize and analyze a cultural pattern imbedded in an anecdote or a brief statement.

Method: In English, provide the examinee with an oral or a written anecdote or statement, and then question the person being assessed.

Question: Is the behavior in this statement typical or atypical for French (French-Canadian, North African, etc.) people? Why? or Why not?

Examples: a) When 15-year old Luc Tremblay and his school friends get together in Québec to play sports, they usually play a game of "boules" (lawn bowling) outside a local café; b) The Dupont family, a typical middle class French family, is going to spend its summer vacation at home in Paris, as usual.

Type 7. A question about the significance of a fact

Purpose: To see if students can infer and explain the significance of geographical, historical, economic, political, or social facts.

Method: Brief answer or multiple choice items can be used.

Examples: a) On a map of France locate the following cities: Paris, Lyon, Bordeaux, and Strasbourg. Explain what geographical feature these four cities have in common, and indicate why these cities developed in their particular locations; b) You have won a trip to five French-speaking countries. Look at the maps of Europe and Africa below. You have 20 seconds to study the maps after which you will hear the question: "Où est-ce que vous allez?" The tone will follow with a pause for you to name in French the five countries you wish to visit. (Reminder: Be sure to select only French-speaking countries. For example, Italy would be incorrect.) Then, give one historical or one cultural fact about each of the countries you wish to visit. Explain the significance of these facts. (Adapted from the Indiana Assessment Tasks)

Type 8. A "culture assimilator"

Purpose: To assess how well an examinee understands the importance of culturally appropriate behavior by a non-native in another culture.

Method: Give the person being assessed the description in English of a situation in which a culture-based problem arises because of improper behavior on the part of the non-native.

Example: Mr. Smith, an American sales representative, sets up an appointment with the director of a French company. When making the appointment, the director's secretary stresses to Mr. Smith that her boss is a very busy man. Therefore, Mr. Smith arrives punctually for the meeting, introduces himself to the director of the firm, and quickly takes a contract proposal out of his briefcase. Mr. Smith's attempt to land this client is doomed to failure.

Questions: a) Why does Mr. Smith's behavior elicit a negative response from the director of the French company? b) How should Mr. Smith have behaved when meeting the director of the French company at the company's offices?

Type 9. A report on reading

Purpose: To assess what cultural information an examinee has been able to learn from reading printed sources.

Method: Ask the person being assessed to prepare and present an oral or a written report (in a test situation or not) on a series of written materials that have been assigned to be read.

Examples: Assign a series of five articles from magazines or journals or chapters from books on the role and function of the drum in the Francophone cultures of Sub-Saharan Africa and the Caribbean, or on the holidays that are celebrated annually in France, or on the pronunciation of French in Québec.

Questions: a) What cutural values, thought patterns, or presuppositions were revealed to you in these readings? Explain. b) What sociolinguistic behaviors of this culture became clear, or more comprehensible to you, through these readings? c) What is the symbolism attached to the drum (or certain holidays, or the concept of "joual") in the culture about which you read?

D. COMMUNICATION IN CULTURAL CONTEXT

Type 10. Simulated interactions or situations

Purpose: To determine if examinees know how to behave and to express themselves appropriately in a cultural situation.

Method: Give the person being assessed a written or an oral situation in English (or French) in which non-natives might find themselves and in which non-native behavior or oral responses might prove embarrassing or misleading.

Examples: a) You are Tom Smith. You are having dinner in Lyon at the home of your friend, Annie Petit. During dessert, M. Petit offers you more "tarte aux fraises."

Tasks: Ask for more dessert. Refuse in an appropriate manner. Use any appropriate gestures to accompany your responses.

b) You are Wendy Miller. You are in Paris, looking for the Louvre, but you are lost. I am the *agent de police* on the corner. Ask me for help.

Tasks: Say something appropriate when you approach the policeman. Ask the *agent* for directions.

c) You are Wendy Miller. You are an hour late in arriving at a restaurant in Tours where you are meeting three French friends for lunch.

Tasks: Say something appropriately apologetic, inventing an excuse, when you arrive. Imagine your friends' sceptical response; describe the gesture that might accompany their response.

Type 11. Cultural significance of underlined words or phrases

Purpose: To be able to assess whether or not an examinee can recognize and explain the significance of French words or phrases and their relationship to a common cultural value, thought pattern, or presupposition.

Method: Give the person being assessed a sentence or a brief paragraph written in French in which culturally significant words or phrases are underlined.

Examples: a) Jean Thévenet prépare avec grande joie son voyage aux Etats-Unis, mais il a peur que *sa famille* lui manque beaucoup.

Question: In the context of this sentence, what cultural value is implied in the underlined words?

b) Il faut faire attention à notre nouveau voisin. Il est vraiment *trop poli pour être honnête.*

Question: What presupposition about human nature does the underlined phrase illustrate?

Type 12. Identification of significant features in a literary passage

Purpose: To have the examinee demonstrate a balance of linguistic, aesthetic, and cultural competence based on an example of literary expression.

Method: Give a short literary passage written in French to the person being assessed. For K–8, a fairy tale or children's poem may be most appropriate; for grades 9–12 and beyond, any literary text, including fairy tales, could serve the purpose.

Example:

— Nicolas, mon petit, nous ne partirons pas avec toi en vacances. Tu iras seul, comme un grand.

— Comment, seul? j'ai demandé. Vous ne partez pas, vous?

— Nicolas, a dit Papa, je t'en prie. Sois raisonnable. Maman et moi, nous irons faire un petit voyage, et comme nous avons pensé que ça ne t'amuserait pas, nous avons décidé que toi, tu irais en colonie de vacances. Ça te fera le plus grand bien. Tu seras avec des petits camarades de ton âge et tu t'amuseras beaucoup (Sempé / Goscinny, *Les Vacances du petit Nicolas*. Paris: Denoël, 1992, p. 78).

Questions: a) What common value, thought pattern, or presupposition can you identify in this passage? Explain your choice(s). b) In this passage, cite one feature or statement that you find interesting from the following points of view: 1) linguistic, 2) literary or stylistic, 3) cultural. Explain each of your choices.

E. ABILITY TO OBSERVE AND ANALYZE A CULTURE

Type 13. A photo or drawing of a situation showing social behavior in an unknown culture

Purpose: To see if students can use the knowledge they have learned about another culture to interpret and analyze the cultural information contained in a picture or a photo.

Method: Show a picture or a photo to those being assessed and ask them to respond to questions of a cultural nature based on the photo or picture.

Examples: Picture of a person at a table using a knife and fork to peel a piece of fruit, an Amerindian peace-pipe ceremony, a Roman soldier with a short sword, or girls playing basketball.

Question: a) What custom can be inferred from this picture?

Type 14. An audio or video document for observation of sociolinguistic behavior

Purpose: To see if students can use the knowledge they have learned about Francophone cultures to interpret the cultural and sociolinguistic information contained in an audio or a video text. At the advanced level, the examinee should be able to sense negative feeling which courtesy veils but does not hide.

Method: Give students a culturally appropriate audio or video selection which allows them to observe and comment upon sociolinguistic behavior within the Francophone culture they are studying.

Questions: a) What sociolinguistic habit can be inferred from this selection? b) Is there more than meets the "ear or eye" in this situation? Explain your response.

Type 15. Organizing and making sense of one's cultural observations

Purpose: To assess students' ability to select and organize appropriate observational techniques which will yield valid insights into the culture. Students should be cautioned not to create stereotypes from limited observations.

Method: Give students questions to respond to based on their own observations of cultural behaviors and have them draw inferences from these behaviors, i.e., organize and make sense out of their observations.

Questions: a) Is it advantageous to keep one's observations in situational context (as in a diary or a journal) or on slips of paper to organize under topics, or both? Why? b) Define briefly some of the cultural values, and one or two habitual thought patterns and some widespread assumptions which affect behavior and social institutions in the culture. How could you best observe these features in the culture?

Type 16. Knowledge of sources of information

Purpose: To assess students' ability to solve culture-based problems and to use appropriate resources to find answers to questions concerning Francophone cultures.

Method: Give students an appropriate literary text, or a film based on a literary text, and have them come up with three to five questions dealing with the sociocultural and/or sociolinguistic context of the work. Then, have students find answers to their own questions using appropriate reference works; i.e., encyclopedias, dictionaries, data bases, etc. For assessment purposes, students should submit their questions, the answers they find to these questions, *and* a bibliography of the works consulted.

Example: Assign Molière's play *Le Bourgeois gentilhomme* to be read by the students. (For grades 4–8, a short story, a one-act play, a poem illustrating aspects of a Francophone culture, a culture-rich section of Dumas' *Les Trois Mousquetaires,* or the Sempé-Goscinny series of "Petit Nicolas" works may be more appropriate.)

Questions (text-based and student generated): Where and when was the play first performed? What was the audience's (or the critics') reaction(s) to the play when it was first performed? How important was the bourgeoisie in 17th-century France? How would M. Jourdain, le "bourgeois gentilhomme," have been dressed in the play? As seen in the play, what are some of the linguistic features that distinguish 17th-century French from contemporary French?

APPENDIX I

To Find Time for Both Language and Culture

Time is our great problem as teachers, not only class time but the time it takes to plan a class period and to be ready with the information involved. A working definition of the essential core begins to solve the problem, just by setting limits. The rest of the solution lies in an arsenal of resources for economizing class time and for finding information. Ten general types of resources are picked for mention here. Workshops and local discussions will easily add more.

1. Motivation sparked by social and cultural topics

Most if not all students today feel involved in some aspect of intercultural conflict or friction with social institutions. Motivation generated by interests and concerns of this kind relate directly to the cultural component, and can spread from there, particularly to literature. It is imperative to leave room for the curiosity of individual students and also of the teacher, whose own interests are contagious. Students need only to be invited to explore in the direction they choose, and the core will take on a personal meaning, for it touches any career interest or hobby.

2. Individualizing a class by personal interests

This device transforms a class into a group of persons interesting to one another. Few subjects give so rich an opportunity to personalize whatever topic arises. Art can become "le domaine de Denise." Geography: Bernard is our explorer. A grammar question, perhaps the teacher herself. Marie is fascinated by history, and Thomas, always the skeptic, asks her why. Real communication results. Concepts associated with a person cease to be abstract, they become easier to remember, and learning is spontaneous.

3. Integrating culture, communication, and grammar

The possibility of mastering the medium of communication by discussing the substance of a discipline is unique to language learning. Meaningful communication is the perfect way to develop communicative competence, and cultural insights drawn from idioms and syntax patterns can make the language and grammar interesting.

The integrated learning of language-and-culture can be visualized as a cube, the four sides representing the language skills—listening, speaking, reading and writing—and the top and bottom representing the grammar and culture. The cube is filled with reinforcing lines from each of the six sides to the other five. From culture to grammar, for example, the history of ideas offers a striking insight into seemingly arbitrary grammatical genders.

Students remember better that abstract nouns are likely to be feminine when they learn that the ancient Greek philosophers, in the early struggle to conceptualize generalization, discovered the simple metaphor of a hen and her chicks, the chicks representing examples. Resources of this kind for integrating language and culture have been collected in Nostrand et al., *Savoir vivre en français,* in Bibliography K, which also uses graphics, "spiraling," and dramatized presentations to enable students to assimilate the value system as they discuss the language and culture in French. It is surprising how soon basic grammar can be discussed in the language, using few grammatical terms.

A prime example of the gain through integration is the chance to teach the value system incidentally, apropos of surface manifestations that students find puzzling. Since the teacher would give some explanation anyway, this need not add to the class time.

Students readily grasp the elements of the system if they are presented incrementally, building toward "main themes" of the culture. Each theme has as its center one of the culture's highest common values, surrounded by the thought patterns and presuppositions which color the meaning of the value.

French individualism, for instance, is supported by the critical habit of mind and the assumption about society which favors the individual above the collective. And French intellectuality involves the habit of seeking a context of relationships, the habit of organizing every product of the mind into a composition, and the assumption that one must see through deceptive appearances to find the inner reality of a person or a situation.

Students prepared by an understanding of the main themes of French culture can appreciate even the culture-dependent humor which occupies a level between high comedy and farce (which are relatively universal). Theodore Mueller found in an experiment at the University of Kentucky that a class which had been taught the 1967 version of these themes laughed where a French audience would laugh—for example, at the intellectual pretensions used by French salesmen to impress buyers—while a control class did not laugh, as they viewed a very culture-specific comedy, Jules Romains' *Docteur Knock.*

4. Live contact with native speakers

Native informants invited for discussion—visiting students, local residents—find students seeking answers to questions that matter to them. The live contact can now take the highly motivating form of deciphering the day's telecasts received by satellite, exchanging e-mail with students in another country, or solving the cross-cultural problems of relations with a sister city—even if no member of the class has yet been abroad.

5. Vertical articulation

Both language learning and understanding of the culture can be made more efficient by a collaborative effort to sequence the process, overcoming the waste of repetition and building on what has already been learned. In both cases, if the receptive ability is developed first, the learner can utilize what has been observed and comprehended as a basis for developing the productive capacity. Sequencing is easier in the study of the culture, which relates to the learner's life experience.

6. Horizontal coordination

Collaboration across the curriculum permits a further gain in efficiency by sharing the burden of the subject matter to be taught, and by making it more coherent for the individual learner. Current events connect with history including the sciences, literature and the arts. History and current events each make the other more meaningful. Grammar, when it is studied in the depth required for learning a language, teaches craftsmanship rather than just correctness.

7. Selection among the culture areas

In the case of the European languages, Eurocentrism can be avoided by arousing enough interest in one other French culture area so that current events will attach to it as they occur.

8. Quick-Information Services

Many rich databases are already accessible in the U.S on the Minitel, ERIC, FRANCIS, etc., and the cost of access to some of them has already become manageabe for a class. Younger and younger students find it fun to satisfy their own curiosity. Teen-agers' projects can be rewarded by publication; for instance, the collecting of cultural insights to make language and grammar interesting, or the identifying of brief film clips to illustrate sociolinguistic patterns.

9. The Repertory of Pedagogical Applications

The project of the Commission's Canadian/U.S. Committee will enable teachers to find the "telling examples" of culture patterns and tested strategies that are being collected: a great saving of time, especially when the repertory takes the form of a database that can quickly answer a question.

10. Added Learning Time

The nine devices above make room for language and culture by using the available time more purposefully and efficiently. A tenth resource is to increase the time available. In addition to the time that students sufficiently motivated will spend on their own individual and group projects, it is possible to increase the class contact time. The contact time can be increased, for example, by asking for "culture lab" hours, on the model of the laboratory sciences, as has been done at Brigham Young University. And in many communities, contact time with native speakers can take the form of exchange lessons with immigrants, help to newcomers in adjusting to American life, translation service for tourists, visits to foreigners in hospitals, organizing a youth group in a sister-city or other bi-national or international organization. Such community services are made the more attractive by the spreading pattern of offering course credit for outreach activities that have educational value.

APPENDIX II

Toward a Deeper Understanding of the French Value System

by Howard Nostrand

1. Motivating Students To Find The Underlying Values

Students judge a foreign culture "weird" when they see only unconnected details. The contrastive "We do this, they do that," if it is used in comparing apparently analogous details of two cultures, merely reinforces ethnocentrism by making the other culture seem to spin off in all directions. It is a Copernican revolution to see that there can be more than one culture with its own center.

The key for an outsider to grasp the coherence of French culture, so evident intuitively to the French, is to become aware of its value system. Students grow interested when they begin to see the whole, as they do when they are gradually acquainted with the values in their context and, particularly, in the light of the practical comments of French researchers on how the values apply in everyday life. Those comments, which conclude this Appendix, enable the teacher to make the succinct definitions on pp. 27–31 much more interesting. But first, let us be well aware ourselves of what is meant by this key to understanding a culture.

2. "A Value System": What The Concept Really Means

Every culture has its own version of individual self-fulfillment and a good society, so that these terms take on different meanings from one culture to the next. Some cultures give priority to the individual, others subordinate the individual to the collective. Each culture, even those which include irreconcilable ultimate beliefs, has a distinctive culture-wide infrastructure, a system which "filters" perceptions, giving to an act or an utterance a meaning which bearers of the culture take for granted. Unwary newcomers assume the meanings to be the same as in their own culture. But as the parts of the system—values, thought patterns, and assumptions—interact with one another, they take on meanings different from what their names suggest to an outsider. This system underlies the culture's seemingly chaotic manifestations at the surface: the social customs, institutions, art forms, idiomatic expressions. Hence the term "infrastructure" (which must not be confused, however, with the Marxist use of that term to mean the class structure and the economic bottom line).

This infrastructure, not economic but social and psychological in nature, has been variously called the culture's ethos, "attitudes profondes," "Weltanschauung," and perhaps best, its "ground of meaning," since it determines the culture-specific meaning of an act or an utterance. Social scientists agree that this infrastructure is made up of a system of shared values—emotionally charged concepts, consciously held when they are used as the criteria for making choices and decisions—and two kinds of mental habit: thought patterns and some prevalent assumptions about human nature and society.

They agree on this despite the different terminologies and despite different approaches. A sociologist like Talcott Parsons, for example, holds that Science must seek universal structures applicable to all cultures, while an anthropologist like Morris Opler maintains that each culture must be described in terms of its own themes, which may be fears of spirits in the forest. When one of a culture's themes is the opposite of a value (for example, a fear), however, it defines a positive value (liberation from that fear), so that both approaches lead to a system of values. A social psychologist such as Alex Inkeles approaches U.S. culture as a cluster of several distinct and equally important personality types, which seems at first to deny that there can be a common infrastructure. But he goes on from there to find that a very large percentage of individuals in each type share a number of common values and assumptions. (See his article in Bibliography B.2).

Social scientists carefully distinguish between the rapidly changing surface patterns, such as the moods of a people—adults as well as adolescents!—which go out of date so soon that they are not worth memorizing, and the stable infrastructure which evolves only at a pace of generations or even centuries. During the past thirty years, the emphasis in French culture has shifted from an ideal of dispassionate reason toward the valuing of emotion; from individualism toward an informal kind of affiliation and interpersonal relationships; and in political attitudes, from a resigned acceptance of politicians as "les responsables" toward the questioning of their capability.

Jacques Paitra elaborates this distinction, for France, in his article, "Opinion et socio-culture." Hélène Riffault's *Les Valeurs des Français* (both are in Bibliography E.2) also shows that the French have thus adapted to the current accelerating social change by finding new forms of their centuries-old values of realism, intellectuality, and rule-circumventing individualism. Hardly ever is a value dropped or added. Rare examples are the glamorous French militarism of earlier centuries, a casualty of modern mass warfare, and the "écologisme" added in response to the rising concern for the environment.

To be sure, the coherence of a culture is always incomplete, because of the constant adaptation to meet new conditions as well as the conflicts to be continually resolved among some of the values—romantic love vs. realism, frankness vs sensitivity, independence vs. sociability—and because of regional and social differences—of gender, generation, politics, and ideology. Outsiders need to be sensitive to these internal differences, but inside and outside observers can complement each other. A culture, like a constellation, has a shape that may best be seen from outside.

The values useful for understanding why people think and act as they do are the culture's "highest common" values, the professed ideals in which people like to recognize themselves. "Highest" means that these values are pursued for their intrinsic merit, not as instruments toward higher objectives. "Common values" means that they are widely shared throughout the population, though in situations that vary with the social differences. These highest common values motivate behavior; they generate the emotional force that drives a choice or a decision. All other common values can be rationally selected as the most effective means toward a higher goal. For example, the thought pattern of logical reasoning is used by the French as a means of carrying out their value of intellectuality. Thought patterns and assumptions, indeed, can always be chosen rationally as instrumental values, though more often still, they are present only subconsciously.

The French commentators in the next section of this appendix caution against the creation of an idealized representation of their culture which would raise false expectations. No culture, in any case, always carries out its ideals, particularly where its values conflict—as in the case of realism and romantic love in French culture. There is also the opposite danger. Many students are prone to disparage a foreign culture, comparing its faults with an idealized version of their own. One needs to point out that this is unfair. It usually turns out, moreover, that the disparaged detail looks different in its true context. It helps to begin early pointing out instances where a detail which looks the same has quite different meanings in the two cultures.

The values actually carried out in everyday life, where they differ from those one intends, can be discovered by research, since the behavior which results from them is observable. In the future, it will be practicable to research the evolution of France and indeed of the whole French-speaking world in the databases, over a hundred, described by Nostrand and Upp (Bibliography D). Six are singled out, on pp. 26–34 of that study, as sufficient for the purposes of the core competence: the U.S. ERIC-CLL, the French FRANCIS, LOGOS, MEMOIRE DE L'EDUCATION, MINITEL, and the Canadian SDM.

3. Recent Comments of French Researchers on the Values Inventory

Validation of the present inventory was begun by first up-dating, with the help of Bibliography E.2, a description produced in 1966–67 from a wide range of sources by a large team under a federal grant, *Background Data for the Teaching of French* (ERIC Document ED 031 964). The up-dated version was submitted in 1994 to 21 prominent French researchers, of whom 18 responded. The inventory has been revised to reflect their emendations, and their comments are reported below. The commentators make the summary definitions in the values inventory come to life as they add concrete applications, nuances, and cautions. Interesting conflicts of opinion appear in several areas; for example, over the relative importance of learning everyday culture or "high culture" (i.e., studying the great minds of the past), and over the question whether French culture is universal and tantamount to civilization, as many would like to believe, or at least "potentially" so, or not so at all.

Sixteen of the eighteen repondents explicitly approve the inventory in its present form, provided one is careful to point out the differences within France according to social class, gender, age group, politics, religion, and geographical region. **Claude LEVI-STRAUSS**, without dissenting from the generalizations, urges that it is not through these abstractions but through the study of the great French thinkers, writers, and artists that one can appreciate French culture. **Joffre DUMAZEDIER**, however, the eminent specialist in leisure patterns, in demanding recognition of this aspect of the culture, distinguishes between everyday cultural phenomena and the great achievements of the elites, past and present. His criticism, summarized below, calls for an emphasis on leisure activities.

Several respondents emphasize the importance of recognizing the differences within France: **Pierre BOURDIEU, Michel CROZIER** (*La Société bloquée*), **Edmond-Marc LIPIANSKY** (*Guide France*), and the sociologist/novelist **Albert MEMMI**. Outsiders need to be sensitive to these differences, as well as to the common infrastructure which affects the meaning of an act or an utterance.

While observers from other cultures are struck by what continues to make the French so French, these researchers stress not only the internal differences but also the changes under way. Individualism and the art of living have changed as the rise of informal relationships and social groups provides new opportunities for self-fulfillment. Intellectuality is tempered by a relaxed acceptance and cultivation of emotion. Yet, as the eminent sociologist **Henri MENDRAS** observes, all these modifications and the powerful influences of foreign cultures are absorbed into a persistent French identity, more solid in one sense than ever; **Jean CUISENIER**, Director of the Musée des Arts et Traditions Populaires, finds, in effect, that the regional differences in the popular culture are diminishing.

Overarching all the differences is a loyalty to the tradition of "La France," which remains an *idée-force* while the term "patriotism" becomes less appropriate as the nation-state loses the capacity to assure individual security. And while the meaning of the French Revolution is in dispute, the Declaration of the Rights of Man remains a reference point for all the French-speaking peoples in the continuing fight for human rights.

Marcel H. BOISOT (retired Maître de Conférences, Ecole Polytechnique) is especially helpful because he is the only one of the eighteen researchers who is an insider to both French and American cultures; his mother was American, and he has been a successful negotiator between the two cultures as head of the firm "M B Consult." He considers the first characteristic of the French "personnalité de base" to be a certain skepticism, often carried to excess, which marks the initial reaction to the unfamiliar. Skepticism relates to intellectuality, perhaps unconsciously: it is associated with independence of mind, and with the ability to grasp the essential in a matter, particularly its weak points.

Intellectuality, he notes, sometimes takes the form of rationalization, a mental construct which is rational only in appearance. It can also take the form of a superficial analysis and synthesis, criticized by the French as much as by outsiders: "a confusion between elegant association and actual proof" (Samuel Johnson), or "the sacrifice of the exigencies of truth to the desire to please or astonish" (Kant).

Boisot insists, secondly, on the contradictions in the French personality. (These Guy Michaud has ennumerated at length in his careful synthesis, re-edited over three decades: see *Nouveau Guide France,* Hachette, 1990, pp. 17–23.) Boisot selects for mention, first, the opposition between Cartesianism and the visionary bent of the Celts; then within the Celtic heritage, a paradox which opposes individualism to the clannish devotion to village, region, race, party, or club; and a sensitivity to a larger humane cause, which relates to a desire to be admired, indeed, to be loved. Love, Platonic or carnal, is central to the French mentality and mores.

Finally, Boisot sees a detriment in the French characteristic which contrasts with the American concentration on an immediate goal. He finds that his countrymen tend to blunt the drive to act by introducing considerations which he calls "parasitical."

Pierre BOURDIEU (Centre de Sociologie Européenne), considers the values inventory well oriented, but like several other respondents, stresses the differences that must nuance the generalizations. He also stresses the pervasive influence of the school culture. In *La Distinction* (Editions de Minuit, 1979) and *La Noblesse d'Etat* (ibid., 1989), he claims it is no accident that the hierarchal social structure, in which the dominating and the dominated both take their situation as given, closely parallels an inculcated cognitive structure which assumes a dualistic pattern of relationships, contrasting the dominant with the subordinate.

Michael CROZIER (SMG France S.A., Paris), finds the inventory excellent but in need of updating—as has now been done—under Individualism, Affiliation, Informality, Emotion, Resourcefulness, and Contextual Thinking / Systems Analysis. He recommended that the treatment of Friendship, Distrust, Tendency to Compartmentalize, and Centralization need similar up-dating to reflect the French response to the pressures of our world in revolution. In connection with the increased openness toward others he adds the development of tolerance, a demand for cooperation, and an impatience in the face of barriers (many of which he had examined in *La Société bloquée,* Paris: Seuil, 1970.)

The great merit to be claimed for the study of the French language and culture in the United States, he proposes, is that it provides the challenge of a different sort of universalism, and thus enables Americans to see in clearer perspective their own originality, their weaknesses, their problems and the possibilities of development.

Jean CUISENIER (Centre d'Ethnologie Française; Musée des Arts et Traditions Populaires) answers "Yes" to all of the inventory except the presupposition of the primacy of the individual over the collective, which he finds true "only in a certain measure: when the collective is in reality a cloak hiding particular projects, interests or concerns." (Cf. Boisot's view that this presupposition of individualism stands in mutual contradiction with other elements in the system.) On conscience as an element of individualism, Cuisenier observes that the French distinguish between situations where honesty must reign and others such as taxes or speed limits, where even concealment is tolerated.

Cuisenier adds comments to his "Yes" on a few of the items. Among the values, he adds on "France": "While the French realize that their value system is not universally shared, they think that it can become so, and can serve as the basis for formulations such as the Universal Declaration of the Rights of Man and of the Citizen [1789]." And on "Realism": "This does not preclude the valuing of 'la prouesse,' valor, an individual achievement." He would add to the values "Hierarchy" ("La Hiérarchie: the recognition of privileges and distinctions according to rank, a value which does not at all conflict with distributive justice").

Among the thought patterns, he adds on "Relationism" that insistence on specifying the scope of a topic goes with a rigorous concern to relate the particular to the universal. Among the presuppositions, on the conception of space he maintains, citing his *La Maison rustique: Logique sociale et composition architecturale* (Presses Universitaires de France, 1991) that private space includes space appropriated by social groups or even by large political entities. While he says "Oui" to the distinction, he finds a continuum in which courtyards, back alleys, gardens are more or less private, and chapels, markets, docks, and ports are more or less social.

Daniel DERIVRY (Groupe d'Etude des Méthodes de l'Analyse Sociologoque), after consulting with **Bernard-Pierre LECUYER**, begins with "well observed, but" too flattering to satisfy the French inclination to self-criticism. He adds that (1) The obsession with excellence and with classifying [applied to persons] makes life a constant "concours" (competition) aiming less to improve oneself than to be classified above others; it makes schooling "un forcing" [an aggressive driving] of young minds, and later contributes to the power system observed by Michel Crozier: one fears the face-to-face with one's immediate superior, who is thus remote and deprived of feedback. (2) The taste for ideology remains constant: what is denounced is the ideology of others. At the level of habits of mind, this taste explains the response to a given problem never by concrete cases but by principles. (3) Privacy, within a very limited, enclosed space, is not a recent evolution, but goes back to the Latin *domus*. The neighborhood has little importance, and the relations within it are very reserved. Friendship, which penetrates into the friend's private space, is rightly characterized as exacting and rare: a French person has very few "amis." (4) While self-criticism alternates with self-glorification, self-flagellation appears to be on the increase. The French talk more about the "crisis" of France than foreign observers do. He recommends the *Anneé sociologique* for 1993, edited by Henri MENDRAS and devoted to "La Sociologie des moeurs."

Joffre DUMAZEDIER (Unité de Formation et de Recherche de Sciences de l'Education, Université René Descartes) criticizes the neglect of leisure activities, which now occupy more time in France than work. The expansion of free time, accelerated by the "events of May," 1968, has modified the values of all generations: it has encouraged the expression of individuality, relaxing prescriptive social and family relations, yet it has also strengthened community, multiplying shared festive events and stimulating a shared concern for the environment. He considers the French values in the inventory to be universal, but differs sharply from Lévi-Strauss in rejecting "the image of France limited to the exploits of the elites."

Claude LEVI-STRAUSS (Collège de France) believes that the reasons for studying French are "the universally recognized clarity, rigor, and precision" of the language, and the access it gives to great thinkers and writers. The taste for French culture is developed through these and the artists of France, not through abstractions about it. (Although this is a timely reminder to appreciate high culture, such appreciation proves not to suffice alone for communicative competence. A great observer of other cultures may see his own as the source, not the object, of analysis.)

Edmond Marc LIPIANSKY (social psychologist, Université de Paris X) adds to the internal differences cited by Memmi and others the differences of ideology, politics, and religion. This does not call into question the present inventory, he continues, but requires that it be nuanced by referring to the existing sociological studies. He recommends particularly the volume edited by Hélène Riffault, *Les Valeurs des Français* (PUF, 1994). He considers fundamental the contrastive approach used in the inventory, e.g., in defining French individualism, and he finds E.T. Hall's approach to the conception of time too schematic to describe a given culture. He co-authored with Guy Michaud *Vers une science des civilisations?* (Hachette, 1981), and meanwhile wrote *L'Ame française, ou Le National-libéralisme* (Paris: Anthropos, 1979), after reviewing forty analyses of the French identity ranging from 1895 to 1974. A revised edition, *L'Identité française: Répresentations, mythes, idéologies* (La Garenne Colombe: Espace Européen, 1991) is out of print.

Marie-Claude MARQUET (Bureau de Documentation, Ministère de la Justice, formerly with La Documentation Française) comments: "The analyses of behavior you propose seem quite true. Two elements to take into account are the difference between Paris and 'province' (the rest of France); and apropos of 'polychronic' time, in the fields of teaching and librarianship, among others, the pressure due to a lack of personnel, with the regrettable result that rushing from one thing to another becomes second nature." (One may point out that the conscientious response to the pressure is due to a well-instilled concern to do what is right.)

Albert MEMMI (retired Professor of Sociology as well as novelist) finds the inventory "very complete, perhaps too much so," and joins in urging the importance of differentiating by class, generation, and gender. He cites the class differences in dress, and the contrast in attitudes toward sex exhibited by his generation and that of the 20- to 30-year-olds. He proposes research on the idea that emotion and sentiments remain the same, but distrusts research based too much on opinion polling.

Henri MENDRAS (Observatoire Français des Conjonctures Economiques) also has nothing to add to the list, which he finds "extremely suggestive." He recommends his *Seconde Révolution Française* (Gallimard, 1988), and he adds a point suggested to him by Pierre Nora: that the democratization of French society has been accompanied, paradoxically, by an aristocratization of mores. Cf. also the recommentation of Daniel Derivry at the end of his response.

Edgar MORIN (Association pour la Pensée Complexe) responds simply that he is "entirely in accord with the text." (The term "pensée complexe" refers to systems analysis. Cf. the comment of de Vulpian on conceptualization.)

Jacques PAITRA (Institut Internationale de Démoscopie, and Cofremca) in his *Tocqueville Review* article of 1993, synthesizes research on sociolcultural change in France, against the context of the twenty long-range international trends identified by Cofremca. That research is an important source of up-dating reflected in the Inventory items on Individualism, Affiliation, Informality, Emotion, Resourcefulness, and Contextual Thinking / Systems Analysis.

Hélène RIFFAULT (Gallup International, formerly with the Institut Français d'Opinion Publique), after several readings in the light of her background, finds herslf "profoundly in agreement" with this analysis. She notes that the distrust of politicians mentioned apropos of individualism applies likewise to the Church as institution, to unions, political parties, and many rules of conduct, for example the status of the couple. On the art of living, she adds that the hierarchy of social positions is much weakened, thanks in large part to the level of education. The volume she has edited, *Les Valeurs des Français* (PUF, 1994) shows the common ground among the sectors of French society studied by diverse specialists.

Alain TOURAINE (Centre d'Analyse et d'Intervention Sociologiques, Ecole des Hautes Etudes en Sciences Sociales), distinguishes between a common *modernity* and differing national processes of social and political *modernization*. He finds distinctively French traits more easily in this socio-political process than in cultural values—a useful distinction which is hidden in English by our inclusive definition of the concept "culture." Within his socio-political category, he finds a durable French trait: the predominace of the political realm and its actors over the social realm and its leaders. This can be traced to the history of democracy in France, where the demands for social rights were linked to the political regime, while the British emphasized the limiting of political power. On the (strictly) "cultural plane," the aristocratic theme (luxury, taste), so strong in France, has taken the form of an influence pervading the culture, instead of surviving in the form of a social class as in Britain (cf. Henri Mendras, above, on "the aristocratization of French mores.") Finally, what Touraine finds to be culturally the most French is the habit of protecting private life from a public life dominated by the state—in two ways: the separation of God and religion from the king, and the naturalism, peasant and bourgeois alike, attributed to the ancestral Gauls, which is aggressively opposed to regulation of the pleasures of life, food, drink, and sexuality.

Alain de VULPIAN (Cofremca, engaged in marketing research centering on sociocultural change) comments on two of the values and one habit of thought. "L'amour" is becoming an exchange, and it integrates the physical, the emotional, and the intellectual better than in the past. "La Patrie," to those for whom it has meaning, is less related to the flag, glory, and the Gallic rooster than in the past. "France" is more of a focus. For those it motivates, it means the "humanisme" (humanitarianism) of France and its systems of Social Security. On the modes of conceptualization, he finds a vogue among intellectuals of thinking in terms of systems, and, more interestingly, even among the simplest people, an apparently rapid shift away from the supposition that there is a single cause and a simple solution—"All you have to do is . . ."

Geneviève ZARATE (Ecole Normale Supérieure de Fontenay / Saint-Cloud) subscribes to the comparison of French and American values, which is supported by principles of the history of mentalities, yet she differs from Derivry in believing that the values defined in the inventory are universal, even friendship and intellectuality. She is engaged in a British/French program with Michael Byram to define cultural competence, under the auspices of the Council of Europe. (Their report is discussed in the review of Michael Byram et al., *Culture Studies and Language Learning,* in *Modern Language Journal* 78 (1994): 247–48.) The Council of Europe program necessarily emphasizes the commonality among the European countries rather than the different cultural identities, while the AATF Commission is concerned both with common ground and with differences, even among speakers of the same language and in the same country. It is significant that the two efforts turn out nevertheless to identify essentially the same elements of sociocultural competence.

BIBLIOGRAPHIES

A. COMMUNICATION IN CULTURAL CONTEXT

Ager, Dennis. *Sociolinguistics and Contemporary French.* Cambridge: Cambridge University Press, 1991.

Examines the sociolinguistic contexts of French both in France and abroad, including language attitudes, language policy, gender and occupational issues, social class, and ethnic minorities.

Calbris, G., and L. Porcher. *Geste et Communication. Une recherche sémiologique de la gestualité co-verbale, à partir de tests interculturels et à support filmique et de milliers d'exemples vécus corroborés par des bandes dessinées.* Paris: Didier, 1969.

Carroll, Raymonde. *Evidences invisibles: Américains et Français au quotidien.* Paris: Seuil, 1987. Translated as *Cultural Misunderstandings: The French-American Experience.* Chicago: University of Chicago Press, 1988.

Situationally-based cross-cultural analyses.

Gardin, B. *et al. Sociolinguistique.* Paris: Presses Universitaires de France, 1981.

Garmadi, J. *La Sociolinguistique: approches, théories, pratiques.* Paris: Presses Universitaires de France, 1981.

Nostrand, Howard L., Frances B. Nostrand and Claudette Imberton-Hunt. *Savoir vivre en français.* New York: John Wiley and Sons, 1988.

Vol 1, *Culture et communication,* proposes different nonverbal features to observe in four successive discussions of any authentic film clip of dialogue: distance between speakers; hands, arms, faces, body, legs, smiles; symbolic versus automatic gestures; rhythm. See pp. 9, 45, 84, 142.

Sanders, Carol, ed. *French Today: Language in its Social Context.* Cambridge, England: Cambridge University Press, 1993.

A collection of articles examining trends in the French-speaking world, including topics such as prescriptivism, gender and language, regional languages and dialects.

Seelye, H. Ned, and Alan Seelye-James. *Culture Clash: Managing in a Multicultural World.* Lincolnwood, IL: National Textbook Co. Business Books, 1995.

For students interested in international careers, concrete experience on, for example: "Communicating Across Different Values," "Dealing With Unspoken Aspects of Culture," "Accepting Ourselves as Culturally Conditioned Beings," and "The Fallacy of Projected Cognitive Similarity." Each chapter offers analyses and solutions of problem situations and ends with a "Tool Kit."

Valdes, Joyce Merrill, ed. *Culture Bound: Bridging the Cultural Gap in Language Teaching.* Cambridge, England: Cambridge University Press, 1986.

See the chapter by Genelle Morain, "Kinesics and Cross-Cultural Understanding," pp. 64–76.

Walter, Henriette. *Le Français dans tous les sens.* Paris: Laffont, 1988.

An historical and sociolinguistic overview of the French language: regional languages, French abroad, language trends.

Wylie, Laurence. "Learning Language and Communication." *French Review* 58, No. 6 (May 1985): 777–785.

A mature synthesis of the sociolinguistic context of verbal and nonverbal communication, including the essential and regrettably neglected rhythmic interaction between speakers.

B. SKILLS OF OBSERVATION AND ANALYSIS

Brown, Ina Corinne. *Understanding Other Cultures.* Englewood Cliffs, NJ: Prentice Hall, 1963.

Presents problems common to all human beings with an explanation of the many different ways various societies approach and solve them.

Byram, Michael, and Geneviève Zarate. *Définitions, objectifs et évaluation de la compétence socioculturelle.* Strasbourg: Conseil de l'Europe, 1993. Modern Language Program, Troisième rapport.

Closely parallels the present report in including methods of analysis, attitudinal outcomes, and sociolinguistics, as well as identifying the core features of a culture (see also Byram in Biblio. J).

Carroll, Raymonde. *Evidences invisibles: Américains et Français au quotidien.* 1987 (see Biblio. A).

Narrates and analyzes interesting situations at the points of conflict between two historically close and relatively similar cultures.

Damen, Louise. *Culture Learning: The Fifth Dimension in the Classroom.* Reading, MA: Addison-Wesley, 1987. Second-Language Professional Library.

An imaginative treatment of the basic topics enables one to browse in intriguing yet instructive byways: the *-emic* vs. *-etic* modes of cultural description; separating the social from the cultural; the Sapir-Whorf hypothesis; cultural identity; Lévi-Stauss and myth; cross-cultural research; culture shock; techniques of cultural training.

Galloway, Vicki. "Toward a Cultural Reading of Authentic Texts." In *Languages For a Multicultural World in Transition.* Ed. Heidi Byrnes. Lincolnwood, IL: National Textbook Co., 1992. 87–121.

Starting from where the learner "is," and applying creative thinking to such exemples as the French opposition between work and leisure, aims at the understanding that there are no simple counterparts between cultures, because each culture has a conceptual framework which gives an anecdote or other text a culture-specific meaning.

Garcia, Carmen. "Using Authentic Reading Texts to Discover Underlying Socio-cultural Information." *Foreign Language Annals* 24, No. 6 (1991): 515–26.

Hall, Edward T. *The Silent Language.* Garden City, NY: Doubleday, 1959.

Here, in his first book, Hall explores the field of kinesics and nonverbal communication, including gestures and body language. Hall also examines cultural differences in societies represented by different uses of time and space, and the values reflected in these living patterns.

_____. *The Hidden Dimension.* Garden City, NY: Doubleday, 1966.

The cultural differences in the conceptualizing of space, including proxemics, personal distancing, and the layout of houses and towns.

_____. *Beyond Culture.* Garden City, NY: Anchor Press/ Doubleday, 1976.

This text is an exploration of the unconscious cultural elements that affect the daily living patterns of people around the world. Hall develops here the key concepts of "high and low context cultures" and "monochronic and polychronic time". Chapter 15 is devoted to the subject of self-identification.

_____. *The Dance of Life: The Other Dimension of Time.* Garden City, NY: Anchor Press/Doubleday, 1983.

An analysis of "time as culture, how time is consciously as well as unconsciously formulated, used, and patterned in different cultures" (p.3). Among cultural differences is the synchronizing of rhythm between interacting persons. A glossary (pp. 209–213) defines Hall's tool concepts.

_____. and Mildred Reed Hall. *Hidden Differences: Studies in International Communication; How to Communicate with the Germans.* Hamburg, Germany: Gruner & Jahr AG & Co., Service de Publicité Stern, 1983. Trans. *Les différences cachées: Une étude de la communication internationale; Comment communiquer avec les Allemands.* Ibid., 1984.

Applies to the French and Germans his method of analyzing differences in communication and business style, and concepts of time, space, power, order, and work ethic. The 10 x 10 grid he devised with George Trager is on pp. 118–19.

_____. and Mildred Reed Hall. *Understanding Cultural Differences: Germans, French and Americans.* Yarmouth, ME:Intercultural Press, 1989.

Concise comparison of themes in the three cultures with an emphasis on business relations.

Kramsch, Claire. *Context and Culture in Language Teaching.* Oxford: Oxford University Press, 1993.

A fresh approach to communicative competence, using discourse analysis. Explains the importance of understanding a) the particular context on which the authenticity of a text or situation depends and b) the context which the student brings to a narrative, a poem, or a social exchange. Chapter 5 deals with "Teaching the literary text"; chapter 6 examines the neglected question, "What is cultural authenticity?" (cf. Galloway, above, and Nostrand, 1989, in Biblio. K).

Nora, Pierre. *Les Lieux de mémoire.* See, in particular, Vol. II: "La Nation." Paris: Gallimard, 1986.

Nostrand, Howard L. "Authentic Texts and Cultural Authenticity; An Editorial." *Modern Language Journal* 73, No. 1 (Spring 1989): 49–52.

Denies that "authentic texts" assure understanding; unless a student is enabled to see a text or a social situation against its authentic cultural background, the authenticity is lost (cf. Kramsch above).

_____. "The 'Emergent Model' (Structured Inventory of a Sociocultural System) Applied to Contemporary France." *Contemporary French Civilization* 2 (1977): 277–94.

Based on a reconciliation, explained in an introduction, between the anthropologist Morris Opler's "main themes" description, specific to a given sociocultural system, and the sociologist Talcott Parsons' organization of the data on values, habits of mind, common assumptions, and also on art forms, the language, and nonverbal communication. The society subsystem includes the family, public institutions, status by sex, socio-economic class and age groups, and social conflict. An environment subsystem includes health. Opler explains his theme-analysis approach in three references cited on p. 310 of Seelye (see below, Biblio. K).

Valdes, Joyce Merrill, ed. *Culture Bound: Bridging the Cultural Gap in Language Teaching.* 1986 (see Biblio. A).

Readable background on cultural analysis, differences and similarities (includes the Third World and China, kinesics, culture shock, and classroom applications).

C. EMPATHY TOWARD OTHER CULTURES

Bellah, Robert N., R. Madsen, W.M. Sullivan, A. Swidler and S.M. Tipton. *Habits of the Heart. Individualism and Commitment in American Life.* New York: Harper and Row, 1985; rpt. Perennial Library, 1986.

This sociology classic can provide American learners of French with an important framework for understanding their own American culture before they try to understand a Francophone culture.

Benadava, Salvador. "De la civilisation à l'ethno-communication." *Le Français dans le Monde* 170 (juillet 1982): 33–38.

_____. "La Civilisation dans la communication." *Le Français dans le Monde* 184 (avril 1984): 79–86.

> Both articles stress a combining of "civilisation" with language teaching rather than as a separate field.

Bourdieu, Pierre. *La Distinction.* Paris: Editions de Minuit, 1979.

> A trenchant sociological analysis of the way in which the French educational system reproduces class distinctions and perpetuates "l'ordre établi"; a critical insider's view of French culture.

Byram, Michael, Veronica Esarte-Sarries, and Susan Taylor. *Cultural Studies and Language Learning: A Research Report.* London: Taylor and Francis, 1991. Multilingual Matters, No. 63.

> This is the fourth book of "The [University of] Durham Project" series (for the first three, and additional information on this item, see Byram *et al.* in section J). Demonstrates interview-research on pupils' perceptions of other cultures, their attitudes toward foreign peoples, and the sources of the stereotypes or other misconceptions which they bring to school. Explains how perceptions, attitudes, and other variables have been given operational form.

Kramsch, Claire. *Context and Culture in Language Teaching.* 1993 (see Biblio. B).

Seelye, H. Ned. *Teaching Culture: Strategies for Intercultural Communication.* 3rd. ed. Lincolnwood, IL: National Textbook Company, 1993.

> Chapter 11 deals with attitudes.

D. FRENCH-SPEAKING AREAS (GENERAL)

For information and materials on an aspect of a given country, to supplement what will be found below or in an encyclopedia, one may contact the country's nearest consulate, or the consulate general or embassy. Any library can find the addresses. Many libraries can also tell how to access two growing electronic resources. The first consists of databases, including the Minitel services and newswire services, from which one can copy bibliographical references and sometimes whole articles. The other is the E-mail "bulletin boards," to which one can send queries that often bring answers volunteered by specialists in the United or another country.

Culturgrams. Brigham Young U, David M. Kennedy Center for International Studies Publication Services, 280 HRCB, UT 84602. Tel. (801) 378-6528. One set of 100+, $40. Quantity prices to non-profit buyers, (800) 528-6275. Individual Culturgrams will be mailed on receipt of $1.00 each. Quotes of over 50 words require written permission; duplicating is forbidden by copyright.

> These experience-based briefings condense in four pages a wealth of practical information in units entitled "Customs and Courtesies" (greetings, visiting, eating, gestures); "The People" (attitudes, clothing, population, languages, religion); "Life Style" (family, dating, diet, business, recreation, holiday); and "The Nation" (climate, history, government, economy, education, transportation, communication, travel, health). Included are Algeria, Belgium, Canada (Quebec), France, Luxembourg, Morocco, Senegal, and Tahiti. To be added are Haiti, Cameroon, and other West African countries.

Délégation générale à la langue française [under the Premier Ministre; replaced the Commissariat général de la langue française, 1939]. Centre de documentaion et d'information, Mme Josseline Bruchet, Chef, 1 rue de la Manutention, 75116 Paris. Tél. 40.69.12.00.

As part of its mission to promote the diffusion and good usage of French and to coordinate the contributing agencies, this center disseminates *gratis* such official documents as: "Troisième Sommet de la francophonie" (essays by heads of state), Editions Mermon, 1989; a summary description and history of cooperation in the French-language community of 44 to 58 countries or areas; glossaries (e.g., computer terms) and bibliographies.

Diagonales. Quarterly Supplement, since 1987, to *Le Français dans le Monde.* Paris: Hachette.

Excellent material, oriented toward teaching, on the cultures and societies of the French-speaking world outside France.

Haut Conseil de la Francophonie. *Etat de la francophonie dans le monde.* Paris: La Documentation Française, 1991.

Based on data and new studies, the 1991 report of the Haut Conseil de la Francophonie addresses various issues pertaining to French-speaking countries: human rights, environmental policies, status of the French language, writers, education, culture, communication, science.

La Francophonie. CNDP, Direction Documentaire, 29 rue d'Ulm, 74230 Paris Cedex 05. Pp. 108, maps. Coll. "Références documentaires," No. 47. Réf. 001 Z3147. 56 F.

History, literature, media, projects of cooperation. Also noteworthy is Réf. 0600 B2049, *Littérature et francophonie,* a special issue of *Ecrire. Ibid.,* 1989. Pp. 120. 70 F).

Kellermann, Luce. *La Dimension culturelle du développement: Bibliographie sélective et annotée.* Paris: UNESCO, 1986. Pp. 378 et Annexes, 25 pp. (In French only.)

Cultural problems and policies of Third World development (chapters II.3 and III–V). See Index of countries, Annexes pp. 23–25, by the longtime documentalist of Paul-Henry Chombart de Lauwe's Centre d'ethnologie sociale et de psychosociologie.

_____. *La Dimension culturelle du développement: Bibliographie sélective et annotée, 1985–1990.* Paris: L'Harmattan, 1992.

See also the annual catalog of L'Harmattan for Afrique noire, Maghreb, Cara_bes, Amériques, Asie, Océan indien.

Luce, Louise Fiber. *The French-Speaking World: An Anthology of Cross-Cultural Perspectives.* Lincolnwood, IL: National Textbook Co., 1991.

Highlights the rich diversity of cultures sharing the bond of a common language; includes discussion questions and student activities. Robert Lafayette recommends (*Modern Language Journal* 76, Autumn, 1992: 415–16) the chapters by Laurence Wylie on French value orientations and several other relatively current chapters, while criticizing the too-inclusive title.

Nostrand, Howard L., and Gerald Richard Upp. *Databases: Our Third Technical Revolution.* Champaign, IL 61820: American Association of Teachers of French, 1991. $10 postpaid.

(The two earlier "revolutions" were audio and AV models.) Over 100 databases, in France, Canada, Germany and the US, constitute the main sources for research-based knowledge of the French-speaking world. The monograph includes information on access to the databases. Research on France and its European setting can be updated through FRANCIS, LOGOS, and MEMOIRE DE L'EDUCATION, edited by the Centre National de Documentation Pédagogique, which incorporates the teaching materials contributed by the CRDP (Centres Régionaux), including France's five Départements d'Outre-Mer. Research on the rest of *la Francophonie* is covered by SDM (Montreal), and BIEF (Ottawa). Pedagogical research is covered in ERIC, MEMOIRE DE L'EDUCATION, and the Informationszentrum für Fremdsprachenforschung (Philipps Universität, Marburg).

Organisations et associations francophones: Répertoire 1989. La Documentation française, 29 quai Voltaire, 75340 Paris Cedex 07. 75 F.

This third compilation lists 318 organizations.

Rhinesmith, Stephen. "Cultural Values and Intercultural Adjustment." In *The French-Speaking World: An Anthology of Cross-Cultural Perspectives.* Ed. Louise Fiber Luce. Lincolnwood, IL: National Textbook Co., 1991.

E. FRANCE

1. General

Albistur, Maïté, and Daniel Armogathe. *Histoire du féminisme français du Moyen-Age à nos jours.* Paris: Des Femmes, 1977.

A clear, comprehensive, and easy to consult historical survey of feminism in France.

Braudel, Fernand. *L'Identité de la France.* Paris: Arthaud; Flammarion, 1986. 2 vols. Translated as *The Identity of France.* Vol 1, *History and Environment.* New York: Harper and Row, 1988; Vol. 2, *People and Production.* London: William Collins Sons, 1990.

In Vol. 1, *Espace et histoire,* this innovative socioeconomic historian traces the diversity of the land from the third millennium B.C. to the development of the nation. In Vol. 1, *Les Hommes et les choses,* Part 1, he retraces the demography and economy from the prehistoric populations to the 20th-century problems of social services, population size, and ethnic relations; Part 2 treats the transition from a peasant economy to 20th-century industry and capitalism. Persistent values are evident in these changing contexts.

Braun, Patrick, and Kamel Lakrouf. *Les Enfants de la terreur.* La Jeunesse dans les banlieues d'aujourd'hui. Paris: Mercure de France, 1993.

An interesting study on violence which has been increasing in the French "banlieues" in the past few years. The development of gangs in France is also addressed.

Carroll, Raymonde. *Evidences invisibles: Américains et Français au quotidien,* 1988 (see Biblio. A).

Cazeneuve, Jean, ed. *Le Grand Livre de la France.* Paris: Larousse, 1988.

Sophisticated coverage of most of the topics we are dealing with are put in a historical perspective in this work.

Corbett, James. *Through French Windows: An Introduction to France in the Nineties.* Ann Arbor, MI: The Univ. of Michigan Press, 1994.

This is one of the best, most up-to-date books on France in the nineties. It is a comprehensive overview of contemporary France that draws on a vast array of journalistic sources. Although very conscious of French modernism and fascination with high-tech, Corbett never loses sight of the conservative perspectives that coexist with modernist tendencies.

Cotentin-Rey, Ghislaine. *Les Grandes Etapes de la civilisation française.* Paris: Bordas, 1991.

This is the new edition of Thoraval's book which presents a survey of French civilization, including not only historical events and literary movements but also artistic achievements, scientific discoveries, and daily life through the ages.

D'Amécourt, M. *Savoir-Vivre.* Paris: Larousse, 1966.

Excellent source on French manners and social customs.

Daninos, Pierre. *La France dans tous ses états.* Paris: Hachette, 1985.

This book, which is written with the same humor as *Les Carnets du Major Thompson,* is a satire of contemporary France, with chapters devoted to specific aspects such as population, vacation and the Club Med, for example.

Debbasch, Charles and Jean-Marie Pontier. *La Société française.* 2e éd. Paris: Dalloz, 1991.

This 900-page panorama, setting current social trends in historical perspective, is a fundamental reference source. It is very complete in its coverage of population changes, national identity, social structures, the family, values and attitudes, religion, gender and age differences, rural and urban oppositions, political life, and the arts.

Dirn, Louis. *La Société française en tendances.* Paris: Presses Universitaires de France, 1990.

Entrer dans le XXIe siècle. Essai sur l'avenir de l'identité française. Paris: La Documentation Française, 1990.

This essay identifies three revolutions (family, work, and education) and examines the conflicts between the individual and the state, as well as France's role in Europe and on the broader international scene.

Duby, Georges, and Robert Mandrou. *Histoire de la civilisation française.* 2 vols. Paris: Armand Colin, 1984.

Excellent survey, by two eminent historians, of French civilization from the Middle Ages to the Mitterrand era. Good bibliographical entries.

L'Etat de la France, 1994–95. Nouvelle éd. Paris: La Découverte, 1994.

In addition to topics covered in Debbasch (above) or Mermet (below), a 200-page "Tour de France des régions" assesses the health of each administrative region with abundant statistics. Other short articles by academics and journalists treat the economy and France's international role. Updated every year.

Frémy, Dominique et Michèle Frémy. *Quid.* Paris: Robert Laffont (updated every year).

This large reference volume contains a wealth of current information on France and other countries on all topics. It includes a substantial index.

Galland, Olivier. *Les Jeunes.* Paris: La Découverte, 1993.

A concise survey of issues facing the youth in France, including an historical development and bibliography.

Garaud, Christian. "Un portrait et des retouches utiles? Les Français dans *Le Nouveau Guide France.*" *Contemporary French Civilization* 18, No. 6 (Summer–Fall 1994): 208–219.

Horn, Pierre L., ed. *Handbook of French Popular Culture.* New York: Greenwood Press, 1991.

Irbarne, Philippe d'. *La Logique de l'honneur.* Paris: Seuil, 1989.

Lapeyronnie, Didier, and Jean-Louis Marie. *Campus blues. Les étudiants face à leurs études.* Paris: Seuil, 1992.

Interesting study on the current condition of college students in France, the university system with its strengths and weaknesses, grievances from students, and possible solutions to current problems; includes data and bibliography.

Mendras, Henri. *La Seconde Révolution française 1965–1984.* Paris: Gallimard, 1988. English adaptation: *Social Change in Modern France: Towards a Cultural Anthropology of the Fifth Republic.* Cambridge, England: Cambridge University Press (and Paris: Editions de la Maison des sciences de l'homme), 1991. Revised ed. *La Seconde Révolution Française, 1965–1984.* Gallimard, 1994.

A fine historical analysis; shows how the social equilibrium which emerged from the Revolution of 1789 has been transformed since World War II. M. Mendras recommends this study from among his writings, and adds a point suggested by Pierre Nora: as French society has grown more democratic, particularly since the 60s, its mores have become more aristocratic (unlike Britain, where aristocracy has remained a class rather than diffusing as an influence). See Nora below.

Mermet, Gérard. *Francoscopie 1995.* Paris: Larousse, 1994.

Covering much the same ground as Debbasch, but with more statistics, attractive graphics, and a more accessible style and format, this book is perhaps the single most useful guide to contemporary France. It is organized around the individual, the family, society, work, and leisure. Updated every other year.

Michaud, Guy, et al. *Le Nouveau Guide France.* Paris: Hachette, 1990.

Millet, Catherine. *L'Art contemporain en France.* Paris: Flammarion, 1987.

A good survey on the topic, including many illustrations.

Nora, Pierre. "Démocratisation de la société, aristocratisation des moeurs." *Le Débat* (Gallimard), 57 (Nov.–Dec. 1989): 175–179.

A centuries-old thought pattern of treating the context of an object as part of its definition, in contrast with the American pattern of treating an object or a situation as self-dependent, even in the rules of legal evidence.

Oger, Armelle. *La Nouvelle Famille.* Paris: Belfond, 1993.

> Based on a study, this book shows how the increasing divorce rate and the decrease of marriage in France has led to a new type of family where the various roles are not well defined; bibliography included.

Pynson, Pascale. *La France à table.* Paris: La Documentation Française, 1987.

> Thorough study on current eating habits in France, supplemented by a wealth of data. It includes the influence of large supermarkets, the role of the dieting craze and popular magazines, social and regional differences.

Rivière, Daniel. *Histoire de la France.* Guides pour tous. Paris: Hachette, 1986.

> There are many books on French history; this particular title offers a short and concise summary on the subject, along with aspects of civilization; many illustrations.

Sarde, Michèle. *Regard sur les Françaises: Xe siècle - XXe siècle.* Paris: Stock, 1983.

> Lengthy historical essay on the position of women in society from courtly love to the MLF. Particularly fine on the relationship between society and literature.

Schnapper, Dominique. *La France de l'intégration. Sociologie de la nation en 1990.* Paris: Gallimard, 1991.

La Société française. Données sociales 1993. Paris: I.N.S.E.E., 1993.

> Updated every three years, this is an excellent collection of articles by specialists, supported by statistics, on the following topics: population, education and professional training, employment, health, the family, budget, social classes, living conditions, social groups, and social benefits.

Vasconcellos, Maria. *Le Système éducatif.* Paris: La Découverte, 1993.

> A concise description of the French education system, including a short historical survey, strengths and weaknesses, and a detailed bibliography.

Welcome, Geneviève and Claire Willerval. *Juniorscopie.* Paris: Larousse, 1986.

> This book should prove particularly useful to French teachers at all levels, as it offers a survey of the lifestyles and concerns of youth in contemporary France.

Wylie, Laurence. *Les Français.* Englewood Cliffs, NJ: Prentice Hall, 1970.

> A new edition of this excellent book is currently being prepared by Jean-François Brière.

Zeldin, Theodore. *The French.* American ed., N.Y.: Pantheon, 1982.

> Chapters discuss individual diversity, humor "and when to look solemn," "love and family relations," "how to compete and negotiate with them," social classes, taste in food and style, language and education, status of women, minorities, and foreigners, and "what it means to be French." The author elicits the comment from a French native, "He understands us better than I do myself." Zeldin contributed two volumes on *France, 1848–1945* (Oxford University Press, 1973–1977) to the *Oxford History of Modern Europe:* Vol. 1, "Ambition, Love and Politics," examined "The pretensions of the bourgeoisie" in chapters on nine professions, marriage and morals, children, and women; Vol. 2, "Intellect, Taste and Anxiety," likewise anticipated themes discussed in *The French.*

2. The French Value System

Braudel, Fernand. *L'Identité de la France.* 1986 (see above, Biblio. E.1, for the socioeconomic perspective).

Dumazedier, Joffre. *Révolution culturelle du temps libre, 1968–1988.* Paris: Meridiens Klincksieck, 1988.

This work criticizes the neglect of leisure activities, which now occupy more time in France than work. The expansion of free time, accelerated by the "événements" of May 1968, has modified how values are applied by all generations. It has encouraged the expression of individuality, relaxing prescriptive social and family relations, yet it has also strengthened community, multiplying shared festive events and stimulating a shared concern for the environment. Dumazedier rejects "the image of France limited to the exploits of the elites" (cf. Hofstede, below, on work-related values).

Garaud, Christian. "Un Portrait et des retouches utiles? Les Français dans *Le Nouveau Guide France.*" *Contemporary French Civilization* 18, No. 2 (Summer/Fall), 1994: 208–224.

Garaud sides with the theorists who reject any generalization about a culture. Indeed, the early uncritical generalization, such as Salvador de Madariaga's on the English, the French, and the Spaniards, must be avoided. Anthony Wallace represents a constructive departure from both that fault and the detriment of rejecting critical generalization, in his synthesis, "The New Culture-and-Personality," on pages 1–12 of *Anthropology and Human Behavior* (Anthropological Society of Washington D.C., 1962). Two decades later he held that the subsequent refinements did not destroy the basis laid in that volume.

Hofstede, Geert. *Culture's Consequences: International Differences in Work-Related Values.* New York: Sage Publications, 1980.

The place of France among 40 countries with respect to four basic variables: male dominance, individualism, power distance in interpersonal relations, and tolerance of amibiguity (the ability to be comfortable with uncertainty, antithetic to the French concern to "voir clair"); cf. Dumazedier, above, on leisure activities.

Lerner, Daniel. "Interviewing Frenchmen." *The American Journal of Sociology* 62 (Sept. 1956): 187–194.

Learner validated a half-century ago an apparent near-constant individualism, a nation-wide self-concept, through the regular response, "You can't learn from me about the French, because we are all so different."

Lipiansky, Edmond Marc. *L'Ame française ou le national-libéralisme: Analyse d'une représentation sociale.* Paris: Editions Anthropos, 1979. Revised ed., *L'Identité française: Représentations, mythes, idéologies.* La Garenne Colombe: Espace Européen, 1991 (out of print).

A University of Paris X specialist in group psychology evaluates the validity of the French self-concept and of French and German views of each other (after reviewing forty main analyses of the French identity, ranging from 1895 to 1974). How different observers organize the persistent characteristics, which they all see, depends on the model they apply: psychological, psychosociological, or ethnic.

Mendras, Pierre. *La Seconde Révolution Française, 1965–1984.* Revised ed., 1994 (see Biblio. E.1).

Nostrand, Howard L. "French Culture's Concern for Relationships: Relationism." *Foreign Language Annals* 6, No. 4 (May 1973): 469–480.

> The tendancy to regard the context of an object as essential for defining it; the opposite of the American view of an object as self-dependent.

Paitra, Jacques. "Opinion et socio-culture: Evolution de la société française, situation en 1992–1993." *Tocqueville Review* 14, No. 2 (1993): 139–155.

> The accelerating sociocultural change defined by the long-range marketing research of COFEMCA has been met by French values which far antedate the 20th century: 1) A society of job insecurity and expected international instability is treated with realism and intellectuality; reasoning has produced attitudes of flexibility between alternative scenarios and has tempered initial extreme reactions (e.g., toward immigrants); 2) New freedom to express one's individuality has broadened the scope of the old two-sided value of individualism/freedom, and in this case reasoning has led to a re-examination of the possibilities of self-management and physical fitness; 3) Dissatisfaction with rigid social conventionalities has given rise to informal community relationships and organizations, calling into play the rule-breaking inventiveness ("débrouillardise") which has long characterized French individualism; in the workplace, one result has been a demand for "autonomy," prompted by the centuries-old concern for the art of living.

Riffault, Hélène, ed. *Les Valeurs des Français.* Paris: Presses Universitaires de France, 1994.

> Based on in-depth interviews in 9 countries of Europe, 1981 and 1990, this study confirms for France the trends noted in the Inventory of the French Value System in Part III.A. above, emphasizing the following: individualization and satisfaction through self-fulfillment; informal, *ad hoc* social structures; the shift from ideology to relativism (such as Pascal's "Truth this side of the Pyrenees, error on the other") and to a pragmatic quest for what is good here and now; and distrust of out-groups, contrasted with a selected in-group.

Zeldin, Theodore. *The French* (see Biblio. E.1).

3. France and Europe

Bryssinck, René, Marina Boudart, and Michel Boudart, eds. *Modern Belgium.* Brussels: Modern Belgium Association, 1990.

> Sixty essays by distinguished contributors. The seven parts include the topics in parentheses: "The Land and the People" (geography, history), "International Policy" (Europe, Atlantic Alliance, Africa), "The Constitutional System and the Interactions of Political Systems," "The Economy" (trends, agriculture, industry service sector, foreign trade), "Social Policy" (labor, welfare, immigration, health), "Education," "Science," "Culture" (French and Dutch literature, the arts, gastronomy).

Evaluation d'une action pour la Dimension Européenne dans l'Education: Le Réseau d'Institutions de Formation. Groupe international d'évaluation. Nantes: Université de Nantes, Nov. 15, 1993.

> The Réseau d'Institutions de Formation (R.I.F.) was established in 1989 by a group of European educators with the support of the Commission of the European Union, in accord with the Treaty of Maastricht, to coordinate the efforts of the participating universities as they develop the European dimension of their teaching and teacher education, in cooperation with the ERASMUS program, the Association for Teacher Education in Europe, and the Commission's own Task force, "Ressources Humaines."

Haenens, Albert d'. *La Belgique. Société et cultures depuis 150 ans, 1830–1980.* Bruxelles: Ministère des Affaires Etrangères, 1980.

> This excellent book presents Belgium under its major aspects, such as geography, population, institutions, economy and social organizations, religions and morals, education and reasearch, cultural practices, and Belgians in the world. It also contains many illustrations.

Koop, Marie-Christine. "Education et formation professionnelle dans l'Europe de 1993." *French Review* 65, No. 6 (May 1992): 891–900.

> Shows how ERASMUS, COMETT, and other cooperative programs are reconciling innovation with the respect for national diversity.

Kummerly and Frey. *La Suisse. Peuple. Etat. Economie. Culture.* Berne: Editions géographiques (updated yearly).

> This little book provides a survey of Switzerland and contains a great deal of information in a concise form. It can be used as an introduction to the study of Switzerland, but should be supplemented by a more thorough analysis.

Paulhan, Jean-Kély. "Citoyen européen?" *French Review* 67, No. 5 (April 1994): 735–745.

> Clarifies the contrast between the two relationships, to France and to Europe.

Tiersky, Ronald. *France in the New Europe: Changing Yet Steadfast.* Belmont, CA: Wadsworth Publishing Co., 1994.

> Ideologies have yielded to the quest for a pragmatic consensus on the problems of adapting to European union, absorbing the eight percent of non-native population, including Moslems, and maintaining the equality of opportunity institutionalized in the welfare state, whose health insurance and nearly free education from infancy through the doctorate, offered to all present, are an increasingly heavy burden.

F. FRENCH-SPEAKING NORTH AMERICA

1. The French Presence in America: The Pre-Nineteenth Century Period

Berthiaume, Pierre. *L'Aventure américaine au XVIIIe siècle. Du voyage à l'écriture.* Ottawa: Presses de l'Université d'Ottawa, 1990.

Breton, Raymond and Pierre Savard. *The Quebec and Acadian Diaspora in North America.* Toronto: The Multicultural History Society of Ontario, 1982.

Coulet du Gard, René and Dominique Coulet Wester. *The Handbook of French Place Names in the U.S.A. 1776–1976.* In *Onomastica*, No. 53. Ottawa: Edition des Deux mondes, 1977.

> Useful study illustrating the wide range of French exlorations.

Eccles, W.J. *France in America.* East Lansing, MI: Michigan State UP, 1990.

Very manageable work which views the French adventure in North America with a great deal of sympathy.

Olivier, Phillipe. *Bibliographie des travaux relatifs aux relations entre la France et les Etats-Unis,* IV. *Souvenirs et présence de la France sur le territoire actuel des Etats-Unis. Les Francophonies américaines.* Paris: Aux Amateurs du Livre, 1990 (Part I); Paris: Klincksieck, 1991 (Part II).

Part I of this bibliography treats works concerning the French presence from Alabama to the Great Lakes and from Maryland to Wyoming; Part II contains works on Louisiana.

Parkman, Francis. *France and England in North America.* The Library of America, vols. 11–12. New York: Literary Classics of the United States, 1983.

One of the best written works in English describing the early French experience in North America.

Thwaites, Reuben Gold. *The Jesuit Relations and Allied Documents. Travel and Exploration of the Jesuit Missionaries in New France 1610–1791.* 73 vols. Cleveland, OH: Burrow, 1896–1901.

2. Quebec

Balthazar, Louis. "The Faces of Quebec Nationalism." *Contemporary French Civilisation* 17, No. 2 (summer–fall 1993): 268–291.

Bessette, Emilie, Réginald Hamel, and Laurent Mailhot. *Répertoire pratique de littérature et de culture québécoises.* Montréal: Fédération internationale des professeurs de français, 1982.

Chartier, Armand B. "French-Canadian Literature: An Introductory Bibliography." *Modern Language Studies* 6 (Fall, 1976): 54–71.

Culturgram for the 1990's: Québec Province of Canada. Brigham Young U, David M. Kennedy Center for International Studies, Publication services, 280 HRCB, Utah 84602. Tel. (801) 378–6528.

Contains, in succinct form, an introduction to Quebec: its customs, people, lifestyle, etc.

Gauvin, Lise. *Lettres d'une autre.* Montréal: L'Hexagone, 1987.

_____. and Laurent Mailhot. *Guide culturel du Québec.* Montréal: Boréal Express, 1982.

Giroux, Robert, Constance Havard, and Rick LaPalme. *Le Guide de la chanson québécoise.* Montréal: Triptyque, 1991.

Lafortune, Monique. *Le Roman québécois, reflet d'une société.* Laval: Mondia, 1985.

Mathieu, Jacques and Jacques Lacoursière. *Les Mémoires québécoises.* Sainte-Foy: Presses de l'Université Laval, 1991.

Murphy, Joseph A. "Quebec Literary Bibliography: A Library Acquisitions Approach." *The French Review* 67, No. 6 (May 1994): 985–1012.

This whole issue of *The French Review* is devoted to Quebec.

Rioux, Marcel. *La Question du Québec*. Montréal: L'Hexagone, 1987.

_____. *Les Québécois*. Paris: Seuil, 1975.

Senécal, André. *A Reader's Guide to Québec Studies*. Québec: Gouvernement du Québec, 1988.

> Valuable bibliography providing a guide to all important aspects of the world of Quebec.

Têtu de Labsade, Françoise. *Le Québec, un pays, une culture*. Montréal: Boréal, 1990.

Wade, Mason. *The French-Canadians, 1760–1945*. Toronto: MacMillan, 1945 (translated as *Les Canadiens-Français de 1760–1945*. 2 vols. Montréal: Le Cercle du Livre de France, 1963).

Weinmann, Heinz. *Du Canada au Québec, généalogie d'une histoire*. Montréal: L'Hexagone, 1987.

3. Current French Presence in the United States

a. General

Creagh, Ronald. *Nos Cousins d'Amérique*. Paris: Payot, 1988.

> Includes short presentations on small groups of French immigrants in recent times who have settled in various parts of the U.S. (e.g. Basques in Nevada and Bretons in New York). This study is also useful in reference to literature written in French by Francophones of African descent (e.g. in Louisiana).

A Franco-American Overview, 6 Vols. National Assessment and Dissemination Center for Bilingual Education: Cambridge, MA, 1979—.

> Intended to help readers develop an appreciation of the contributions of Franco-Americans to the cultural heritage of the United States.

Francophonies d'Amérique. Ottawa: Les Presses de l'Université d'Ottawa, 1991 (No. 1); 1992 (No. 2).

Freeman, Stanley L., Jr. and Raymond J. Pelletier. *Manuel du Professeur pour Introduire les Etudes Franco-Américaines. Initiation to Franco-American Studies: A Handbook for Teachers*. Orono, ME: Canadian/Franco-American Studies Project, 1981.

Gilroy, James P. *Francophone Literatures of the New World*. Denver, CO: U of Denver Occasional Papers, No. 2, 1982.

Louder, Dean and Eric Waddell. *French America. Mobility, Identity, and Minority Experience Across the Continent*. Trans. Franklin Philip. Baton Rouge and London: Louisiana State University Press, 1993.

Péloquin, Louise, ed. *Foyers francophones aux Etats-Unis*. Paris: Didier Erudition, 1988. In *Etudes de linguistique appliquée,* nouvelle série (avril–juin 1988).

Savary, Claude, ed. *Les Rapports culturels entre le Québec et les Etats-Unis*. Québec: Institut québécois de recherche sur la culture, 1984.

Tessier, Jules and Pierre-Louis Vaillancourt, eds. *Les autres littératures d'expression française en Amérique du nord.* Ottawa: Editions de l'Université d'Ottawa, 1987.

Viatte, Auguste. *Histoire littéraire de l'Amérique française: des origines à 1950.* Québec: Presses de l'Université Laval (and Paris: Presses Universitaires de France), 1954.

_____. *Anthologie littéraire de l'Amérique francophone.* Sherbrooke, Québec: Faculté des Arts, 1971.

Waddell, Eric and Dean Louder. *Du continent perdu à l'archipel retrouvé. Le Québec et l'Amérique française.* Québec: Les Presses de l'Université de Laval, 1983.

b. The Franco-Americans of New England

Anctil, Pierre. *A Franco-American Bibliography.* Bedford, NH: National Materials Development Center for French, 1979.

This work and others listed below produced by the NMDCF can be obtained from the Centre Franco-Américain, 52 Concord St, Manchester, NH 03101.

Brault, Gérard J. *The French-Canadian Heritage in New England.* Hanover, NH: University Press of New England; Kingston and Montréal: McGill-Queen's University Press, 1986.

Chartier, Armand. *Histoire des Franco-Américains de la Nouvelle-Angleterre, 1775–1990.* Sillery, Québec: Editions du Septentrion, 1990.

Doty, C. Stewart. *The First Franco-Americans.* Orono, ME: University of Maine at Orono Press, 1985.

Louder, Dean. *Le Québec et les Francophones de la Nouvelle-Angleterre.* Sainte-Foy: Presses de l'Université Laval, 1991.

Series of articles on work which has been done in this area with suggestions for work to be done in the future.

Pélquin-Faré, Louise. *L'Identité culturelle. Les Franco-Américains de la Nouvelle Angleterre.* CREDIF. Paris: Didier, 1983.

Poteet, Maurice. *Textes de l'exode. Recueil de textes sur l'émigration des Québécois aux Etats-Unis (XIXe et XXe siècles).* Montréal: Guérin littérature, 1987.

Quintal, Claire, ed. *The Little Canadas of New England.* Worcester, MA: The French Institute of the Collège de l'Assomption, 1982; *Le Journalisme de langue française aux Etats-Unis. Ibid.,* 1983; *Les Franco-Américains et leurs institutions scolaires. Ibid.,* 1990; *La Littérature franco-américaine: écrivains et écritures. Ibid.,* 1991; *La Religion catholique et l'appartenance franco-américaine. Ibid.,* 1993; *La Femme franco-américaine. Ibid.,* 1994.

Very useful studies resulting from the proceedings of the annual meetings of the French Institute of the Collège de l'Assomption in Worcester, MA.

Roby, Yves. *Les Franco-Américains de la Nouvelle-Angleterre, 1776–1930.* Sillery, Québec: Editions du Septentrion, 1990.

Roche, François. *Les Francos de la Nouvelle-Angleterre. Anthologie franco-américaine (XIXe et XXe siècles).* Co-edition LARC—Centre d'Action Culturelle, Le Creusot et Langes, Cultures et Communication. Paris: Les Belles Lettres, 1981.

Santerre, Richard. *Anthologie de la littérature franco-américaine de la Nouvelle-Angleterre.* 9 vols. Bedford, NH: National Materials Development Center for French, 1981.

Viau, Eusèbe, ed. *Chants populaires des Franco-Américains.* 12 vols. Woonsocket, RI: Union Saint-Jean-Baptiste d'Amérique, 1925–1942.

Weil, François. *Les Franco-Américains, 1860–1980.* Paris: Belin, 1989.

c. The French Presence in Louisiana

Allain, Mathé and Barry Ancelet. *Littérature française de la Louisiane. Anthologie.* Bedford, NH: National Materials Development Center for French, 1981.

Dural, Carolyn. *Bibliographie des écrits louisianais français de 1900 jusqu'à nos jours.* In Tessier, Jules et al. *Les autres littératures . . .* (see Biblio. H.3.a).

Hamel, Réginald. *La Louisiane créole littéraire, politique et sociale, 1762–1900.* 2 vols. Ottawa: Editions Leméac, 1984.

Good overview of French/Cajun culture.

Richard, Zachary. *Voyage de nuit, Cahier de poèsie, 1975–79.* Center for Louisiana Studies Publications (U of South West Louisiana). Lafayette, LA: Editions de la Nouvelle Acadie, 1987.

d. The French Presence in Other Parts of the United States

Examples taken from materials compiled by Philippe Olivier for all states and territories (see above, this Biblio., H.1).

Illinois:

Brouillette, Benoît. *La Pénétration du continent américain par les Canadiens Français, 1763–1846. Traitants, Explorateurs, Missionnaires.* Montréal: Granger Frères, 1939; rpt. Montréal: FIDES, 1979.

Sutton, Robert P., ed. *The Prairie State. A Documentary History of Illinios.* 2 vols. Grand Rapids, MI: William B. Eerdmans, 1976.

South Carolina:

Childs, St. Julien Ravanel. "French Origins of Carolina." *Transactions of the Huguenot Society of South Carolina* 50 (1945): 22–44.

Hirsch, Arthur Henry. *The Huguenots of Colonial South Carolina.* Durham: Duke UP, 1928.

Primer, Sylvester. "The Huguenot Descendants in Ante-Bellum South Carolina." *Transactions of the Huguenot Society of South Carolina* 52 (1947): 24–37.

G. FRENCH-SPEAKING SUB-SAHARAN AFRICA AND THE CARIBBEAN

Ackerman, Hans W. and Jeannine Gauthier. "The Ways and Nature of the Zombi." *Journal of American Folklore* 104, No. 414 (Fall 1991): 466–494.

Nice analysis of folklore: zombi, Haiti, Africa, and a bibliography on other folktales. Given the importance of oral language, story-telling, and tales such as the Ananse Tales, this article should be read by anyone seeking greater insights into African institutions.

African Studies: African Outreach Series #6

The University of Illinois at Champaign-Urbana is a good source of slides, films, and other materials, 1208 West California (Room 101), Urbana, IL 61801. Phone: (217) 333–6335. Inquire about their *Afrique en français* catalogue.

L'Atlas Jeune Afrique du continent africain. Paris: Editions du Jaguar, 1994.

The first reference atlas on Africa. The first part contains a general approach to the African continent: political map, geography, history, Africa in the world, the economy, and social issues. The second part devotes a section to each African country. Informative and very attractive with 200 color maps. Preface written by Léopold Senghor.

Brooks, Lester. *African achievements: leaders, civilizations, and culture of ancient Africa.* Stanford, CT: De Gustibus Press, 1992.

An excellent resource book for both teachers and high school students to use in investigating cultural and historical information on Africa. While the focus is on ancient Africa, it is an important resource for anyone interested in the African notion of time as focusing on both past and present.

Clark, Leon E. *The Present—Tradition and Change.* New York: CITE Books, 1989.

An excellent reference book for teachers who desire to understand African perspectives, particularly as seen in today's international world. It is a book which readers will find enlightening.

Culturgram for the 1990's: REPUBLIC OF SENEGAL. Brigham Young University, David M. Kennedy Center for International Studies, Publications Services, 280 HRCB, Provo, UT 84602. Tel. (801) 378-6528.

An excellent four-page resource on Senegal for teachers; contents include customs and courtesies, the people, lifestyles, and the nation. Other francophone countries are included in forthcoming documents.

Ekeh, Peter P. "Social Anthropology and Two Contrasting Uses of Tribalism in Africa." *Comparative Studies in Society and History* 32, No. 4 (Oct. 1990): 660–700.

A good overview of important aspects of African history, ethnology, social history, ethnic groups, slave trade, and African colonization. This book is particularly important for those wishing to understand African society and social routines as a basis for *francophonie*.

Fanon, Frantz. *Les Damnés de la terre.* Paris: T. Maspero, 1968.

An anti-colonial perspective which includes information on France's colonization of Africa as well as a description of offenses against the people. Many of Fanon's usual themes are found in this work.

Fottorino, Eric, Christophe Guillemin, and Erik Orsenna. *Besoin d'Afrique.* Paris: Artheme Fayard, 1992.

> An informative treatment of Africa for anyone interested in a contemporary analysis of Africa and modern views of the African Diaspora. Of particular interest are the brief section of Aimé Césaire and the final section on "avenirs d'Afrique."

Geertz, Clifford. *Local Knowledge: further essays in interpretative anthropology.* New York: Basic Books, 1983.

Georget, Thérèse. *Contes des Antilles.* Paris: Nathan, 1990.

> This collection of stories by different authors is a wonderful resource for the teacher who wants to make available to advanced and superior proficiency students the rich resources of Francophone literature. The stories include a text illustrated with drawings, end-notes for the student, and questions to check comprehension.

Hughes, Langston. *Anthologie africaine et malgache.* Paris: Editions Seghers, 1978.

> A nice collection of essays on African literature translated from the French and French literature from African languages.

Kesteloot, Lilyan. *Anthologie négro-africaine: panorama critique des prosateurs, poètes, et dramaturges noirs du XXe siècle.* Verviers: Marabout, 1981.

> An excellent background reference for those interested in Francophone African literature. Both commentaries and sample poems and stories are included.

Manning, Patrick. *Francophone Sub-Saharan Africa, 1880–1985.* Cambridge, England: Cambridge UP, 1988.

Senghor, Leopold S. *Poèmes.* Paris: Seuil, 1964.

> A collection of some of Senghor's most successful poems, many of which illustrate his frequent themes: mother earth, the tam-tam (drum symbolism), difficulties of returning to one's native Africa after living in Europe, relating to the earth. Poems written during two different periods of Senghor's life as well as a miscellaneous section are included.

SPICE (African Project), Lou Henry Hoover Bldg, Room 200, Stanford University, Stanford, CA 94305-2319.

> An excellent set of modules for teachers who wish to emphasize Africa in their French curriculum. The units are written in English with suggested classroom activities for students. They are particularly useful for middle and high school learners. For lists of available modules, call (415) 497–1114.

Spronk, Johannes. "Introducing Culture through the Use of Francophone Literature." *Hands on Language.* Vol. 5. Corvallis, OR: Oregon State UP, 1993. 26–36.

> Figure 3 lists ten contrasts between French and African culture (p. 33).

Sunkuli, Leteipa Ole. *A Dictionary of Oral Literature.* Nairobi: Heinemann Kenya, 1990.

> A good source of information on various terms and information related to African folk literature and of particular interest to the reader who wants to learn more about oral traditions which have been maintained despite "modernization."

Zusy, Anne. "The Frontiers of History (carving up Africa)." *New York Times Book Review* 28 Feb. 1988: 12.

An informative short article on African colonization.

H. FRENCH-SPEAKING NORTH AFRICA

Abbas, Farhat. *La Nuit coloniale.* Paris: Julliard, 1962.

Ageron, Charles R. *Les Algériens musulmans et la France. 1870–1919.* Paris: Presses Universitaires de France, 1968, 2 Vols.

Al-Fasi, Allal. *The Independence Movements in Arab North Africa.* NY: Octagon Books, 1970.

L'Atlas Jeune Afrique du continent africain (see Biblio. F).

Berque, Jaque. *Le Maghreb entre deux guerres.* Paris: Seuil, 1962.

Boudiaf, Mohamed. *Où Va l'Algérie?* Paris: Editions de l'Etoile, 1964.

Bourguiba, Habib. *La Tunisie et la France.* Paris: Julliard, 1954.

Brown, Leon Carl. "Tunisia under the French Protectorate: A History of Ideological Change." Dissertation Harvard University., 1962.

Brunschwig, Henry. *French Colonialism, 1871–1914. Myths and Realities.* NY: Praeger, 1966.

Burgat, François. *L'Islamisme au Maghreb.* Paris: Karthala, 1988.

Dejeux, Jean (Père). *Le Dictionnaire d'auteurs maghrébins de langue française.* Paris: Karthala, 1984.

Dermot, F. Murphy. "Colonial and Post-Colonial Language Policy in the Maghreb." *The Maghreb Review* 2, No. 2 (1977): 1–9.

Despois, Jean et René Raymond. *Géographie de l'Afrique du Nord-Ouest.* Collection Bibliothèque Scientifique. Paris: Payot, 1967 (43 maps and figures).

Dozy, Reinhart P. A. *Essai sur l'Histoire de l'Islamisme.* Amsterdam: Oriental Press, 1966.

Duclos, Louis-Jean, Jean Duvignaud, and Jean Lecas. *Les Nationalismes maghrébins.* Collection Etudes maghrébins 7. Paris: Fondation des Sciences Politiques, 1966.

Fanon, Frantz. *Les Damnés de la Terre.* 1968 (see Biblio. F).

Ganiage, Jean. *Les Origines du Protectorat français en Tunisie, 1861–1881.* Paris: Presses Universitaires de France, 1959.

Gordon, David. *North Africa's French Legacy*. Harvard UP, 1964.

Grandguillaume, Gilbert. "Les Conflits de l'Arabisation." *The Maghreb Review* 10, No. 2–3 (1985): 57–61.

Hermassi, Abdel-Baki. *Leadership and National Development in North Africa: A Comparative Study*. Berkeley: U of California P, 1972.

Lacoste, Camille, and Yves Lacoste, eds. *L'Etat du Maghreb*. Paris: La Découverte, 1991.

Collection of essays by specialists on all aspects of the Maghreb: history, politics, the economy, social issues, daily life, arts and culture.

Laroui, Abdallah. *L'Histoire du Maghreb. Un Essai de Synthèse*. Collection Textes à l'appui. Paris: Maspero, 1970.

Lazrag, Marnia. "The Reproduction of Colonial Ideology: The Case of the Kabyle Berbers." *Arab Studies Quarterly* 5, No. 1 (1983): 380–395.

Marais, Octave. "La Classe dirigeante au Maroc." *Revue Française de Science Politique* 14, No. 4 (Aug. 1964): 709–737.

Memmi, Albert. *Portrait du colonisé, précédé du portrait du colonisateur*. Paris: Buchet/Chastel, 1957.

Micaud, Charles *et al*. *Tunisia, the Politics of Modernization*. NY: Praeger, 1964.

Monego, Joan Phyllis. *Maghrebian Literature in French*. Boston: Twayne Publishers, 1984.

Sarter, Heindemarie and Kamila Sefta. "La Glottopolitique algérienne. Faits et Discours." *Französisch Heute* (June 1992): 107–117.

Said, Edward. *Orientalism*. New York: Vintage Books, 1979.

Suliman, Hassan Sayed. *The Nationalist Movements in the Maghreb: A Comparative Approach*. Uppsala: Scandinavian Institute, 1987.

Waterbury, John. *Le Commandeur des croyants*. Paris: Presses Universitaires de France, 1970.

I. ENGLISH-SPEAKING UNITED STATES

Bellah, Robert N., *et al*. *Habits of the Heart: Individualism and Commitment in American Life*, 1986 (see Biblio. C).

A serious yet popular exposition of American national characteristics, focusing on an individualism markedly different from the French variety.

Commager, Henry Steele. *Meet the USA*. Revised ed., New York: Institute of International Education, 1970.

A brilliant historian's briefing for visitors from abroad.

Inkeles, Alex. "National Character Revisited." *The Tocqueville Review* 12 (1990–1991): 81–117.

A rigorous study in which a social psychologist solves the problem of describing the culture of a nation which contains subgroups, by recognizing a plurality of personality types within it. Statistically, these are "modes of distribution of personality variants." Since his first study of the problem in 1954, research technology and resources have come to make possible this more accurate, pluralistic description of a sociocultural system, which then permits the authentication of culture-wide characteristics, as well as verifiable cross-cultural comparisons.

Inkeles finds that despite the diversity within the USA, 74% to 98% of North Americans agree on the values of competition, the work ethic, and fair rules, and on the assumption that one's achievement depends on oneself. He expects research under way to substantiate up to ten such "realms of agreement in the American public."

Charles William Morris, in *Varieties of Human Value.* (U of Chicago P, 1956), demonstrated the same research method, identifying "13 ways to live" common in different proportions to the United States, Japan, and other nations. He went on to devise a billiard-ball model to represent the antagonistic or supportive relations among the values in a value system.

Kloppenberg, James T. "Republicanism in American History and Historiography." *The Tocqueville Review* 13 (1992): 119–136.

An examination of the genesis of the present conflicts in the value system, e.g., individualism vs. both egalitarianism and humanitarianism.

Lipset, Seymore M. "Two Americas, Two Value Systems: Blacks and Whites." *The Tocqueville Review* 13 (1992): 137–176.

Conclusions drawn by a consummate analyst of opinion polls, concerning the state in the 1990's of the value conflicts within the mainstream, as well as the contrast between ethnic groups. A model of the synthesis one would like for the cultures whose languages we teach.

Seelye, H. Ned. *Teaching Culture. Strategies for Intercultural Communication*. 1993 (see Biblio. C).

See, in particular, "Cultural Values of Americans," pp. 127ff. and "If I'm Bicultural, Will the Real Me Please Stand Up," pp. 235ff.; and more in the index.

Stewart, Edward C. and Milton J. Bennett. *American Culture Patterns: A Cross-Cultural Perspective*. Rev. ed. Yarmouth, ME: Intercultural Press, 1991.

A succinct description from the perspective of a psychologist who has studied Japanese culture as well as cultures of the West.

Williams, Robin M. *American Culture: A Sociological Interpretation*. 3rd revised ed. New York: Knopf, 1970.

This edition devotes 100 pages to the value system. Two decades later, the author finds little change in the relative constants studied.

J. FOREIGN LANGUAGES AND INTERCULTURAL EDUCATION

Note: This large topic includes the area of "Empathy" (see Biblio. C). For the French contribution to understanding intercultural relationships, one will find further engaging reading in any writings locally available by the sociologist Pierre Bourdieu (e.g., *Actes de recherche en sciences sociales* 59 (1985): 86–93, on the search for French traits in 18th century fairy tales), the anthropologist Claude Lévi-Strauss (e.g., *La Pensée sauvage,* on habits of mind, 1962, or *Mythologies,* 1964–71), the pioneering social historians of *Les Annales,* and the historian of French and English ideology Maurice Mauviel (e.g., in proceedings of ARIC—see second item, below).

Allen, Wendy, Keith Anderson, and Léon Narvaez. "Foreign Languages Across the Curriculum: The Applied Foreign Language Component." *Foreign Language Annals* 25 (1992): 11–19.

>Discusses the teaching of the foreign language and its culture in social science departments: a form of integration proposed as an alternative to including the full cultural component in the foreign-language sequence.

ARIC (Association pour la Recherche Interculturelle), Professeur Marguerite Lavallée, Secrétaire, Ecole de Psychologie, Pavillon F.-A. Savard, Université Laval, Sainte Foy, Québec, Canada G1K 7P4. Annual dues, $50 Canadian or 600FF.

>Publishes proceedings of its international meetings, and a *Bulletin,* of which no. 19 (Sept. 1992) reviews studies on cultural identity and values, intercultural conflict and education, and teacher preparation.

Buttjes, Dieter and Michael Byram, eds. *Mediating Language and Culture.* London: Taylor and Francis, 1990. Multilingual Matters, No. 60.

>Compiles theoretical studies, research on student perceptions of several cultures, and teacher-training programs from several European countries.

Byram, Michael. *Cultural Studies in Foreign Language Education.* London: Taylor and Francis, 1989. Multilingual Matters, No. 46.

>The first of the series based on "The [University of] Durham Project," which researches all aspects of language teaching for an intercultural rather than a near-native objective, requiring equal attention, it is argued, to language and culture.

Byram, Michael and Veronica Esarte-Sarries. *Investigating Cultural Studies in Foreign Language Teaching. Ibid.,* 1991. Multilingual Matters, No. 62.

>A companion volume to No. 63 (see below), addressed to teachers and curriculum builders. It begins with the proposed model and comments on the implications of the research findings for teaching and curriculum development.

Byram, Michael, Veronica Esarts-Sarries, and Susan Taylor. *Cultural Studies and Language Learning: A Research Report. Ibid.,* 1991. Multilingual Matters, No. 63.

>Reports research on the effects of language-and-culture learning, based on observation of classrooms in two secondary schools. Critiques four models of culture studies, and, as a bridge from research to curriculum development, proposes an "ideal model" (p. 382); see Biblio. C.

Byram, Michael, and C. Morgan. *Teaching-and-Learning Language-and-Culture. Ibid.,* 1993.

Chapter 5 reports interview-research on "Assessing cultural learning"; examines the problem of assessing attitudinal outcomes as well as knowledge and behavioral skills, and the problem of defining levels of sociocultural competence.

ERIC Clearinghouse on Languages and Linguistics, the Center for Applied Linguistics (CAL), 1118 22nd Sr., N.W., Washington, DC 20037.

Academic libraries have microfiche texts with abstracts and descriptors. Besides tailor-made searches of the database, performed by CAL or at a local library, CAL publishes standardized searches, periodically updated, such No. 201, "Teaching Cross-Cultural Sensitivity in the Language Classroom" (98 items as of June, 1992).

Gudykunst, William B., and Young Yun Kim. *Communicating with Strangers: An Approach to Intercultural Communication.* Reading, MA: Addison-Wesley Publishing Co., 1984.

Cross-cultural communication differs only in degree from communication between persons of different subcultures. This perspective reduces the tendency to stereotype speakers of a foreign language (cf. Singer, below, this Biblio.).

Kellerman, Luce. See above, Biblio. D, her Chapter II.1.3 for training of emissaries to the Third World.

Nostrand, Howard L. "Language Learning and the Perils of Pluralism." *Canadian Modern Language Review* 45, No. 4 (May 1989): 703–714.

Common ground among belief groups cannot be found at the high level of the ultimate sanction of values and ultimate explanation of reality, but can be found at two lower levels, more restricted in content: shared working principles and shared dissatisfactions with the *status quo.*

Preston, Dennis R. *Sociolinguistics and Second Language Acquisition.* Oxford, U.K.: Blackwell, 1989.

Chapter 3 describes in detail the interactional factors of setting, content, and the interpersonal relations involved when interlocutors differ in language and culture.

Roberts, Linda Pavian. "Attitudes of Entering University Freshman toward Foreign Language Study: A Descriptive Analysis." *Modern Language Journal* 76, No. 3 (Autumn 1992): 275–283.

The relative motivating interests of students entering Michigan State U., as evidenced by a project of essays on the reasons for their interest: 80.6% of them cited the benefits derived from study of the culture; the second most common reason, business, was cited by 47.7%.

Robinson, Gail L. *Crosscultural Understanding.* New York: Prentice-Hall, 1988.

One of the best discussions relating this concern to language education. The author is Director of LARC, the federally supported Language Acquisition Resource Center at San Diego State U.

Singer, Marshall R. *Intercultural Communication: A Perceptual Approach.* Englewood Cliffs, NJ: Prentice-Hall, 1987.

Identity groups within a culture have a latent common ground in their way of perceiving reality, which suggests that it is fruitful to look for any similarities as well as differences between cultures.

K. INTEGRATING LANGUAGE AND CULTURE

ACTFL (American Council on the Teaching of Foreign Languages). *Provisional Proficiency Guidelines.* Hastings-on-Hudson [subsequently Yonkers], N.Y.: ACTFL, 1982.

_____. *Proficiency Guidelines. Ibid.,* 1986.

Omits the specific cultural components of 1982, pending further research. This definition of language proficiency is the basis for coordinating student progress in the language and culture as far as proves possible.

Collaborare: News of Academic Alliances in Foreign Languages and Literatures, School/College Faculty Cooperatives. Ellen Silber, Executive Editor, Marymount College, Box 1386, Tarrytown, New York 10591–3796.

Vol. 7, Nos. 2 and 3 (Spring 1992), titled "Close Encounters of a Literary Kind: Teaching Language in Context," features the importance of literature for understanding a culture. The establishing of local academic alliances, bringing school and college teachers together to work on such problems as articulation, has spread nationally from foreign languages to other subjects.

Crawford-Lange, Linda M., and Dale Lange. "Doing the Unthinkable in the Second-Language Classroom: A Process for the Interaction of Language and Culture." In *Teaching for Proficiency, the Organizing Principle.* ACTFL Foreign Language Education Series. Ed. Theodore V. Higgs. Lincolnwood, IL: National Textbook Co., 1984. 139–177.

This work maintains that culture is a process in which language and culture interact and examines the relation to general and global education.

Damen, Louise. *Culture Learning: The Fifth Dimension in the Classroom.* 1987 (see Biblio. B).

Gibaldi, Joseph, ed. Introduction to *Scholarship in Modern Languages and Literatures,* 2nd ed. New York: Modern Language Association of America, 1992.

Chapters by Dennis Baron, "Language, Culture, and Society"; Giles B. Gunn, "Interdisciplinary Studies" and "Ethnic and Minority Studies"; and by Henry Louis Gates, Jr. and David Bathrick, "Cultural Studies."

Hammerly, Hector. *Synthesis in Second Language Teaching: An*

Introduction to Linguistics. Blaine, WA: Second Language Publications, 1982.

See chapter 20 in particular, "Toward Cultural Competence," which relates the problems and methods of this component to those of achieving fluency and accuracy.

Henning, Sylvie Debevic. "Assessing Literary Interpretation Skills." *Foreign Language Annals* 25, No. 4 (1992): 339–355.

A "Literary Interpretation Scale," pp. 344–5, describes tasks which progress from description to anaylysis and from a self-oriented to a world-oriented perspective. The descriptors are organized in eight groups. In a preceding version, the groups are paired together and each pair is assigned to a proficiency level: the same four levels as are used for cultural competence.

King, Charlotte P. "A Linguistic and a Cultural Competence: Can They Live Happily Together?" *Foreign Language Annals* 23, No. 23 (1990): 65–70.

Kramsch, Claire. *Context and Culture in Language Teaching.* 1993 (see Biblio. B).

Examples drawn from classroom experience show how cultural awareness can be developed through the structures of the language.

———. "The Cultural Discourse of Foreign Language Textbooks." In *Toward a New Integration of Language and Culture.* Ed. Alan J. Singerman. Middlebury [subsequently Colchester], VT: Northeast Conference on the Teaching of Foreign Languages, 1988. 63–88.

Across dialogues, pattern drills, and readings, the culture that is constructed in foreign language textbooks is more often than not the native culture of the learner, not the attitudes, values, and topics of concern of the target culture.

Lafayette, Robert C. "Integrating the Teaching of Culture into the Foreign Language Classroom." In *Toward a New Integration of Language and Culture. Ibid.* 47–62.

Lafford, Barbara A. and Michèle Shockey, eds. *Culture and Context: Perspectives on the Acquisition of Cultural Competence in the Foreign Language Classroom.* Monograph Series No. 4. Tempe, AZ: Southwest Conference on Language Teaching, 1993.

See, especially, Gail Guntermann and Gail L. Robinson on teaching the culture; Claire Kramsch on a seminar where teachers from different cultures interact.

Nostrand, Howard L., Francis B. Nostrand, and Claudette Imberton-Hunt. *Savoir vivre en français,* 1988. Vol. 1, "Culture et communication." Vol. 2, "Analyse et application; Cahier de l'étudiant" (see Biblio. A).

The relative constants of French culture and institutions, with the changes under way, in the format of an intermediate college and third-year high-school or Advanced Placement textbook. In 30 tapes, two individualistic French presenters discuss the ideas, and "walk through" reading and grammar lessons. An *Index socioculturel* (pp. 413–18 of vol. I) outlines the references to France and the Francophone world, as well as to methods and concepts for cultural analysis, and international career interests.

Omaggio-Hadley, Alice C. *Teaching Language in Context.* 2nd. ed. Boston: Heinle & Heinle, 1993.

A comprehensive methodology, from definitions of terms and criticism of approaches (e.g., the functional/notional) to activities for review and discussion. Chapter 9, "Teaching for Cultural Understanding," relates the cultural component to the goal of proficiency.

Oxford, Roberta L. "Culture Learning for Language Students: Encouraging Initiative and Interest Through the Cooperative." *Northeast Conference on the Teaching of Foreign Languages Newsletter* 32 (Fall 1992): 13–16.

The author's model "Heritage Project" utilizes small-group, experiential learning. Two to four students are grouped according to responses selected from a wide range of interests listed on a Preference Sheet. The teams produce monthly "Updates," then present their finished projects in the home setting of a "Heritage Evening," using the language (Russian in this case) as far as possible. Grades can be given to teams or to individuals.

Porcher, Louis. *Manières de classe.* Paris: Alliance Française/ Didier, 1987. Series "Fenêtre sur cours."

Methodology developed by the CREDIF (Centre de Recherche et d'Etude pour la Diffusion du Français) applied to class use in high school or college. French texts on universal topics, such as water, animals, plants, or time, are used to show how this language and literature give a culture-specific flavor. Improves on the "daily routine" topic common in U.S. textbooks by illustrating and discussing the management of social, family, and individual time.

Seelye, H. Ned. *Teaching Culture: Strategies for Intercultural Communication.* 1993 (see Biblio. C).

A rich source of ideas for application in the classroom. Chapters 1 and 2 are particularly recommended. Among the subjects not dealt with in other sources is bilingualism.

Singerman, Alan J., ed. *Toward a New Integration of Language and Culture.* Middlebury [subsequently Colchester], Vermont: Northeast Conference of the Teaching of Foreign Languages, 1988.

Includes semiotic and sociolinguistic paths to understanding culture; cultural discourse of textbooks; mass media, authentic documents, video; study abroad and local resources.

Steele, Ross, and Andrew Suozzo. *Teaching French Culture: Theory and Practice.* Lincolnwood, IL: National Textbook Co., 1993.

This study synthesizes the state of the art of developing intercultural competence through understanding of a second culture and society, and advances reasons for selecting the French language area. It goes beyond the present vanguard in developing the concept of the learner as mediator between two cultures, and in analyzing the difficulty of teaching a "high-context" culture—one where hidden assumptions shape the impact of an act or an utterance.

Valdes, Joyce Merrill, ed. *Culture Bound: Bridging the Cultural Gap in Language Teaching.* 1986 (see Biblio. A).

Readable, practical chapters. Part I on language, thought, and culture; Part II on cultural differences and similarities; Part III on classroom applications. The gap is bridged, for example, by the editor's own chapter on "Culture in literature," and by the chapter on culture analysis by Nelson Brooks and George Hughes.

L. ADAPTATION TO GRADES K-8 AND 9-12

"Adolescence in the 1990s: Risk and Opportunity." Special issue of the *Teachers College Record.* Spring, 1993.

Based on multidisciplinary research, a study of what is necessary for healthy adolescent growth at a time of significant social change and distress.

Alexander, W., and C. K. McEwin. *School In the Middle: Status and Program.* Columbus, OH: Middle School Association, 1989.

A succinct summary of characteristics of middle school learners and special needs of transescents. Summary of philosophy of the middle school and the type of curriculum needed to meet the needs of this age group.

Behmer, Daniel E., ed. *"Le Kiosque" Cultural Mini-Skit. A Teaching Unit on French Cultural Patterns.* Detroit: University Publications, 1972.

This unit is composed of three major parts: the pre-viewing preparation, the viewing of the mini-skit in a variety of manners, and the post-viewing follow-up activities. The teaching unit can be adapted for all teaching levels.

Beilin, Harry, and Peter Pufall, eds. *Piaget's Theory: Prospects and Possibilities.* Hillside, NJ: L. Erlbaum Associates, 1992.

Chapters by the continuers who have modified the body of theory; for example, Piaget's view that cognition must precede grammatical structure (cf. the French valuing of intellect). See also Chapman, below, as well as Donaldson for grades K–8 and Keating for grades 9–12.

Bouraoui, Hédi A. *Creaculture: An Interdisciplinary Approach to French Language, Culture, and Literature.* Center for Curriculum Development, 1971.

Two volumes with this title and a third volume, *Parole et Action,* are especially recommended for teachers as valuable for developing a better understanding of French culture and, by comparison and contrast, of our own culture.

Bourque, Jane M. *The French Teen-ager.* Detroit: American Foreign Language Teacher Publications, 1973 (Advancement Press of America, Inc., P.O. Box 07300, Detroit, MI 48207).

Resource and guide to supplement grades 9–12 with information regarding French teenagers in the areas of family, education, dress, leisure time, dating, and politics; a chapter on techniques for teaching culture (mini-drama, visuals, cultural assimilators).

Carroll, John B. "Foreign Languages for Children." *National Elementary Principal* 30 (May 1960): 12–15.

Chapman, Michael. *Constructive Evolution: Origins and Development of Piaget's Thought.* Cambridge, England: Cambridge UP, 1988.

A definitive intellectual biography. See also Beilin, above, as well as Donaldson (grades K–8) and Keating (grades 9–12) below.

Curtain, Helena, and Carol Ann Pesola. *Languages and Children—Making the Match.* New York: Addison-Wesley, 1988.

Theoretical issues and practical suggestions designed to acquaint teachers at elementary/junior high levels with a variety of methods and approaches to teaching a second language to children. Emphasis on curriculum planning and development for active classroom.

Damen, Louise. *Culture Learning: The Fifth Dimension in the Language Classroom.* 1987 (see Biblio. B).

This text explores the use of culture general and culture specific approaches in the foreign language classroom. Opportunities to apply new concepts are offered in the text.

Donaldson, Margaret. *Children's Minds.* New York: Norton, 1978.

The most accessible of the books on Piaget. See also, above, Beilin and Chapman on cognition in children, as well as Keating (grades 9–12) below.

ERIC Clearinghouse on Languages and Linguistics (see Biblio. J).

Mermet, Gérard. *Francoscopie 1993*. 1993 (see Biblio. E).

George, Paul A., Chris Stevenson, Julia Thomason, and James Beane. *The Middle School—And Beyond*. Alexandria, VA: Association for Supervision and Curriculum Development, 1992.

Up-to-date statement of middle-school goals and curriculum needs to meet those goals.

A Guide to Proficiency-Based Instruction in Modern Foreign Languages for Indiana Schools. Indiana Department of Education. Center for School Improvement and Performance. Indianapolis, IN: Division of Curriculum, 1986.

Proposes learning outcomes and instructional scenarios for nine areas of activity for discussion.

A Guide to Proficiency-Based Instruction in French for Indiana Schools. Indiana Department of Education. Center for School Improvement and Performance. Indianapolis, IN: Division of Curriculum, 1987.

Supplemental volume to the preceding entry.

Jay, Charles and Pat Castle, eds. *French Language Education: The Teaching of Culture in the Classroom*. Springfield, IL: Illinois State Department, 1971 (Office of the Superintendent, 316 South Second Street, Springfield, IL 62706).

Collection of essays about the importance of incorporating culture in meaningful ways into elementary and secondary schools. Especially noteworthy: Nostrand, H.L. and F. B. Nostrand, "Culture-Wide Values and Assumptions as Essential Content for Levels I to III," pp. 48–63; Smithson, Rulon N., "French Culture and Civilization for American High School Students," pp. 80–87.

Kaltsounis, Theodore. "Democracy's Challenge as the Foundation for Social Studies." *Theory and Research in Social Education* 22, No. 2 (Spring 1994): 176–193.

The emphasis proposed, with a subtopic for each grade from K to 12, provides a substantive framework for the sequential study of the nature of democracy—in the United States, in the developed and the developing French-speaking countries—and the role and self-interest of the developed countries in the spread of democracy.

Keating, Daniel P. "Adolescent Thinking." In *At the Threshold:The Developing Adolescent*. Ed. S. Shirley Feldman and Glen R. Elliott. Cambridge, MA: Harvard UP, 1990. 466–489.

A particularly up-to-date account of adolescent psychology at puberty, including Piaget's contribution.

Kramsch, Claire. *Context and Culture in Language Teaching*. 1993 (see Biblio. B).

Kurk, Katherine C. *et al. L'Année en français: Un Calendrier perpétuel*. National FLES* Commission of the American Association of Teachers of French, 1994. AATF, 57 E. Armory, Champaign, IL 61820. Spiral bound. $10 postpaid.

Each date commemorates at least one person, briefly identified, or one event, largely of France but occasionally of the other Francophone countires. Eleven full-page drawings, many suitable for overhead or enlargement, by children from first to eighth grade. A Teacher's Guide relates selected activities to various topics, from comic strips, fairy tales, and sports to the French-speaking world. The last page lists the 365 saints' days.

Ladu, Tora Tuve. *Teaching for Cross-Cultural Understanding.* Raleigh, NC: Dept. of Public Instruction, 1968.

Excellent resource for teachers who seek to increase knowledge and understanding of French and Spanish culture. Good delineation of values of French culture (defined with references for teachers); explanations of words not translatable directly to English (e.g., "individualisme," "intellectualité").

_____. *What Makes the French French.* Detroit: American Foreign Language Teacher Publications, 1974 (Advancement Press of America, Inc., P.O. Box 07300, Detroit, MI 48207).

Good resource for succinct information on French culture and an excellent guide for what should be taught and where to find information about various cultural topics. Highlighted in this volume are ecology, social structures, French mentality, art forms, and language.

Lambert, Wallace E. and Otto Klineberg. *Children's Views of Foreign Peoples: A Cross-national Study.* New York: Meredith, 1967.

Lange, Dale. "The Language Teaching Curriculum and a National Agenda." *Foreign Language Instruction: A National Agenda.* In Richard D. Lambert, ed. Special Issue of *The Annals of the American Academy of Political and Social Science* 490 (1987): 70–96.

Several designs related to curriculum development are examined, and the need for the integration of the several contents of language programs is developed. A national agenda for a different direction is offered.

Lorenz, Eileen and Myriam Met. *Teaching Culture in Grades K–8: A Resource Manual for Teachers of French and Spanish.* Rockville, MD: Montgomery County Public Schools, 1994.

Luce, Louise Fiber. *The French-Speaking World: An Anthology of Cross-Cultural Perspectives.* Lincolnwood, IL: National Textbook Company, 1991.

Designed to increase cross-cultural awareness in students and deepen their understanding of Francophone cultures worldwide; includes discussion questions and activities for students (see above, Biblio. D).

Mantle-Bromley, Corinne. "Preparing Schools from Meaningful Culture Learning." *Foreign Language Annals* 25, No. 2 (1992): 117–27.

Met, Myriam. "Learning Language through Content: Learning Content through Language." *Foreign Language Annals* 24 (1991): 281–295.

The focus in this article is on balancing language in its cultural context with further language practice, and on the corollary of coordination with other subjects.

The Middle School We Need: A Report from the ASCD Working Group on the Emerging Adolescent Learner. Washington, D.C.: Association for Supervision and Curriculum Development, 1975.

A thorough guide outlining needs of transescent learners and the restructuring of curriculum needed to address these needs.

Miller, Dale J. *French Teaching Aids.* Provo, UT: Brigham Young University Press, 1972.

Excellent teaching aids in area of French gestures, cuisine, proverbs, cognates, writing skills, and grammar; illustrations.

Miller, Dale J. and Maurice Loiseau. *USA France Culture Capsules.* Culture Contrast Company, 1974.

Cultural Aids for the French classroom teacher. Emphasis on promoting intercultural understanding. "Student Activities" section makes concrete suggestions to better relate own experiences to those of France. Includes authentic texts and numerous illustrations. Topics include food and drink, relationships, distinctive traits, transportation, institutions.

Moeller, Aleidine J. "Literature: A rich resource for teaching language and culture in context." In *Creative Approaches to Teaching Foreign Languages.* Central States Conference Reports. Ed. William N. Hatfield. Lincolnwood, IL: National Textbook Company, 1992. 32–49.

Good resource for concrete strategies for why and how to teach literature in the beginning and intermediate classroom to optimize active use of language while building a shared cultural frame of reference with the target culture.

National Council for the Social Studies. "In Search of a Scope and Sequence for Social Studies." *Social Education* (October 1989): 376–385.

The theme prevalent in the U.S. for each grade, K to 12, described on pp. 380–382, favors interface with FL study: in kindergarten, the diversity of ethnic origins; 1st grade, the family; 2nd, the local community; 3rd, other communities; 4th, the state, its geographical setting compared with others; 5th, history of the United States in some international context; 6th, world cultures; 7th, world history; 8th, the United States, 9th, economics; 10th, government; 11th, United States history; 12th, world problems. See the critique by T. Kaltsounis, above.

Nerenz, Anne G. "The Exploratory Years: Foreign Languages in the Middle-Level Curriculum." In *Shifting the instructional focus to the learner.* Ed. Sally S. Magnan. Middlebury, VT: Northeast Conference on the Teaching of Foreign Languages., 1990. 93–126.

Excellent history of teaching of foreign languages in the middle school and summary of variety of approaches used to date; information on specific needs of transescents and how proficiency approach to teaching can be incorporated at this level.

Nostrand, Howard L. "The Beginning Teacher's Cultural Competence: Goal and Strategy." *Foreign Language Annals* 22, No. 2 (1989): 189–93.

Omaggio, Alice C. *Teaching Language in Context.* 1993 (see Biblio. K).

Pesola, Carol Ann. "Culture in the Elementary School Foreign Language Classroom." *Foreign Language Annals* 24, No. 4 (Sept 1991): 331–346.

Seeyle, H. Ned. *Teaching Culture: Strategies for Intercultural Communication.* 1993 (see Biblio. C).

Steele, Ross and Michel Paoletti. *Civilisation française quotidienne.* 2nd edition. Paris: Hatier, 1986.

Steele, Ross, and José Pavis. *L'Express: Aujourd'hui la France.* Lincolnwood, IL: National Textbook Co., 1993.

Selected texts, with explanations and communication exercises in French, on French attitudes, life styles, the generations; 15 pages on *la Francophonie.* K–12 teachers could use parts as a source book; e.g., students in the upper grades have found a commmon bond with the French in the attitude of concern for the environment (pp. 171–189).

Suozzo, Andrew G. Jr. "Once More with Content: Shifting Emphasis in Intermediate French." *The French Review* 54, No.6 (Feb. 1981): 405–11.

An attempt to present a coherent image of France by using hierarchy as an integrating concept.

Teacher Handbook Second Language Studies K–12. North Carolina Competency-Based Curriculum. Raleigh, NC: Division of Communication Skills, Instructional Services, 1985.

Tiedt, Pamela L. and Iris M. Tiedt. *Multicultural Teaching: A Handbook of Activities, Information and Resources.* Boston, MA: Allyn and Bacon, 1979.

Welcome, Geneviève and Claire Willerval. *Juniorscopie.* 1986 (see Biblio. E.1).

M. TESTING AND EVALUATION

Bartz, Walter H. *Testing Oral Communication in the Foreign Language Classroom.* Language in Education: Theory and Practice Series, No. 17. Washington DC: Center for Applied Linguistics, 1979.

_____. "Are They Learning What We're Teaching? Assessing Language Skills in the Classroom." In *Focus on the Foreign Language Learner: Priorities and Strategies.* Central States Conference Reports. Ed. Lorraine A. Strasheim. Lincolnwood, IL: National Textbook Co., 1991. 69–81.

_____, ed. *French Level I and II Assessment Tasks.* Indianapolis: Indiana Department of Education, 1993.

Buttjes, Dieter, and Michael Byram (see Biblio. J).

See their studies (British) for the evaluation of student attitudes and of changes due to language study.

Byram, Michael. *Cultural Studies in Foreign Language Education.* 1989 (see Biblio. J).

Dandonoli, Patricia. "ACTFL'S Current Research in Proficiency Testing." In *Defining and Developing Proficiency: Guidelines, Implementations, and Concepts.* ACTFL Foreign Language Education Series. Ed. H. Byrnes and M. Canale. Lincolnwood, IL: National Textbook Co., 1987. 75–96.

Garcia, Carmen. "Using Authentic Reading Texts to Discover Underlying Sociocultural Information." 1991 (see Biblio. B).

Lafayette, Robert and Renate Schulz. "Evaluating Cultural Learnings." In *The Cultural Revolution in Foreign Languages: A Guide for Building the Modern Curriculum.* Ed. Robert C. Lafayette. Lincolnwood, IL: National Textbook Co., 1975. 104–18.

Nostrand, Howard I. "Empathy for a Second Culture: Motivations and Techniques." *Responding to New Realities.* ACTFL Foreign Language Education Series, Vol. 5. Ed. G. A. Jarvis. Lincolnwood, IL: National Textbook Co., 1974. 263–327.

Osgood, Charles E. and G.J. Suci. "Factor Analysis of Meaning." *Journal of Experimental Psychology* 50 (1955): 325–38.

Seelye, H. Ned. *Teaching Culture: Strategies for Intercultural Communication.* 1993 (see Biblio. C).

Deals with testing attitudes and understanding.

Shohamy, Elena. "Connection Testing and Learning in the Classroom and on the Program Level." In *Building Bridges and Making Connections.* Northeast Conference Reports. Ed. June K. Phillips. Middlebury [subsequently Colchester], VT: Northeast Conference on the Teaching of Foreign Languages, 1991. 154–78.

Steele, Ross, and Andrew Suozzo. *Teaching French Culture: Theory and Practice.* 1994 (see Biblio. K).

See pages 120–135 on testing instruments, particularly for assessing sensitization to the target culture, as well as factual knowledge. The list of fifteen "types of questions" on pages 131–135, developed by Howard Nostrand, has been revised and expanded in the present report (see Part VI, Testing Cultural Competence).

Valdman, Albert. "Testing Communicative Ability at the University Level." *ADFL Bulletin* 13 (1981): 1–5.

Valette, Rebecca. "The Culture Test." In Rebecca M. Valette. *Modern Language Testing: A Handbook.* 2nd ed. New York: Harcourt Brace Jovanovich, 1977. 263–277.